What The Professionals are Saying ...

FIT FIRST RESPONDERS

First Responders come into their respective professions with a passion. They take written and physical tests, attend academies that require mental and physical perseverance and look forward to life as a member of a noble occupation. Unfortunately our bureaucratic government systems do little to encourage a continuation of this dedication to the self. Too often our physical and emotional well-beings suffer. Jonathan Conneely (Coach JC) and his Fit First Responders program is the answer to this ever growing and dangerous problem. Everything necessary for a life-changing experience you will find in FFR. This book should be a must in every academy in the country. Every veteran should dedicate themselves to it's principles

Lt. Jim Glennon (ret)
Owner of Calibre Press

Coach JC talks it, walks it, and lives it out everyday. He is a walking testament to the power of a disciplined positive life. His zeal for winning at life is infectious and I am grateful he is sharing some insight to illumine the lives of those who serve us everyday-our first responders. Winning all the time is what Coach JC is about, and by sharing his heart through this book I know others will be encouraged as well!

T.W. Shannon
Former Speaker of the Oklahoma House of Representative
www.TWShannon.com

The role of the first responder is one of the most varied and demanding jobs It has been suggested that we are the most fortunate and unfortunate of persons. I can only speak to the life of a firefighter, and we would argue we are the most fortunate consistently. As such, we often feel so grateful and blessed that we are embarrassed by our good fortune and driven to be our best always.

Therefore, we find ourselves obligated to be in our best physical, emotional, and spiritual condition to meet the needs and expectations of the communities in which we serve and exceptional men and women we stand with every day.

Over the course of my career, I have seen many workout and wellness programs and have been tasked, on several occasions, to measure them for my department. I can say without reservation that FIT FOR DUTY and FIT FOR LIFE is in a league of its own.

Coach JC has covered every aspect of wellness, physical fitness, personal growth, spirituality, and duty. The book provides the reader with insight and wisdom as well as practical routines for conditioning to be functionally fit and ready for duty. Coach JC understands fitness is more than strength and conditioning, it is mental readiness and wellness, it is nutrition, and it is community.

Coach JC's FIT FOR DUTY and FIT FOR LIFE book gives your conditioning meaning and purpose. There are many programs and many coaches available for serious first responders who understand the risks and rewards of our chosen professions and, none the less, report for duty.

Chief Bobby Halton ret.
Editor in Chief *Fire Engineering* Magazine
Education Director FDIC International
Editorial Director *Fire Rescue and Fire Apparatus and Emergency Equipment* magazines

Jonathan Conneely, 'Coach JC' is the BEST LIFE COACH I know! He has a heart to help people WIN in LIFE in every aspect. I have seen his passion to help people succeed and have experienced his motivation in my own life, which has changed me for the better. This book will help you WIN, not just in fitness, but in your relationships and will catapult your walk with God as well. As a pastor, I encourage every first responder, citizen and pastor who sees this to make an investment in your life and someone else's life with this book.

Paul Daugherty
Senior Pastor
Victory Christian Center

Tulsans get to live the best lives we can because of first responder heroes like you. You watch out for us, and I am so thankful that Coach JC has dedicated himself to watching out for you. His Fit First Responders program is changing lives in Tulsa. And it is all here for you in this book - how to be your best physically, mentally, emotionally, spiritually, and professionally.

G.T. Bynum
Mayor
City of Tulsa, Oklahoma

Fit First Responders has been invaluable to the Tulsa Fire Department. We appreciate what FFR has done in reducing injuries and creating camaraderie within our department.

Chief Ray Driskell
Tulsa Fire Department

This book is invaluable for our first responders, those who risk their lives every day for us and keep our city streets safe. Coach JC is a master at mindset and gives you an easy to follow, winning game plan to improve all areas

of your life. Coach JC's program is transforming first responders' lives all over the country!

Senator Dan Newberry
Oklahoma District 37
www.DanNewberry.com

Most firefighters come into the profession fit for duty and
excited and passionate about their new careers in the fire
service. Over the years, however, many find that this career
of high stress, unpredictable sleep, physical labor, firehouse
food, and life in general has wreaked havoc on their bodies,
both mentally and physically. FFR is a positive, challenging
fitness program aimed at pushing the most fit firefighter to
strive to be even better and motivating the most out-of-shape
FFR combines fitness, nutrition, positive thinking, and spirituality, and the impact it has made on many of the firefighters
in our department has been life changing! I personally love
seeing the positive attitude changes and the relationships that
have been built between our city's firefighters, medics and
police officers simply by coming together, sweating together, and finishing a challenging workout together. FIT FOR
DUTY, FIT FOR LIFE is a lifesaving concept tailored specifically for those in the profession of saving lives!

Greta J. Hurt
District Chief
Tulsa Fire Department

Coach JC has discovered a proven program for helping the
people who help us. Throughout my time with the City of
Tulsa, I have seen the many hardships our men and women
in the police and fire departments go through. Fit First Responders is the BEST program for strengthening the mind,
body and spirit of a first responder. We all know these
heroes must be emotionally ready, physically able, and mentally prepared for every call that comes in; this program not
only helps them win on the job, but WIN AT LIFE as well.

Whether you have two or twenty years on, this is the best comprehensive program a first responder can find.

Drew Rees
Chief of Staff
Tulsa City Council

Working with First Responders for the last decade, I have come to realize that these men and women are the best of the best. They are ready to answer the call when the lights come on and the sirens begin to wail. They are trained for every situation they will face in the line of duty: How to put out a fire in a 30 story building or how to talk a man down from a radio tower 125 feet in the air. They are trained how to re-start a heart that has stopped beating and to free an individual in an intense hostage situation. We train our First Responders how to respond while on duty, no one however is trained on what to do when the bunker gear comes off and the gun belt is unhooked. No one is training them how you talk to your wife or husband after you have seen the death of a child or a young mom that has overdosed on an illegal drug. Coach JC has put together a winning program that leads First Responders to deal, in a healthy way, with all of the stress that comes from a life of saving others while too often neglecting themselves. This book is a MUST for every man and woman who is putting their life on the line every day for their community. There is not another man in the country that is more committed to seeing our First Responders become Fit for Duty – Fit for Life. Coach JC has answered the call and is responding to the need that he has seen and is taking care of our Heroes.

Chaplain Danny Stockstill
Tulsa Police and Fire Chaplaincy Corps

In twenty years of firefighting, I have been trained to deal with almost any emergency imaginable. What I was never trained in was how to prepare my mind to be able to handle the daily grind of being called to our citizens' worst days and the stress of meeting the expectation of always being my best in a career where an off day could mean the difference between life and death. These stresses bleed over into many first responders' families, marriages and the career that we love, causing discord, divorce, burnout and even suicide. With FIT FIRST RESPONDERS, Coach JC has developed a game plan that finally gives first responders the practical tools that will help them win in life. As they implement these 25 lessons, they will begin to train their mind to be FIT FOR DUTY. FIT FOR LIFE, and the communities they serve will benefit as their fit first responders are prepared to be THE BEST during their citizens' worst.

Greg Ostrum
Assistant Chief
Jenks Fire Rescue

FIT FOR LIFE STORIES

FFR has given me hope! I have struggled with food addiction my whole life. Through this program, I now have the support system in place to conquer my addiction and be my best! FFR has given me my life back! I haven't felt this good since I was in my twenties! I will be fit for duty and fit for life!

Sgt. Keith Prince
Catoosa Police Department

FFR has allowed me to forge relationships with several first responders from different agencies across the state, that I would have likely never met, otherwise. Those relationships have held me accountable and have pushed me to another level physically, mentally, and spiritually. Not only has FFR provided me an environment to strengthen myself, but I find myself pushing others to be the best version of themselves. The coaches at FFR have taken the time to get out into the field and see what first responders deal with on a daily basis. FFR coaches understand the struggles first responders face on and off the job and are 100% sold on getting all of us FIT FOR DUTY and FIT FOR LIFE.

Luke Flanagan
Field Training Officer
Tulsa Police Department

This program has taken me on a journey of self-awareness and accountability. FFR has fostered a new mindset for not only myself, but my entire family. As a "Fit For Life" husband and father, I am better equipped to be what my family needs. As a "Fit For Duty" fireman, I am stronger mentally and physically and adequately prepared for the new challenges I face as a first responder. If you're a first responder in today's world of negativity and attacks, do not miss the opportunity to plug into a program that can change the trajectory of the rest of your life!

Michael Rudick (Rudi)
Fire Engine Operator

I had lost my faith a long time ago. My first month at FFR, as a coach spoke to the group, something inside of me said I had to find my faith again. I went to church after a 20-year hiatus and embraced the love of God again. It REALLY IS FIT IN ALL ASPECTS OF LIFE! MENTALLY, PHYSICALLY, EMOTIONALLY, and SPIRITUALLY.

Samantha Evans
Advanced EMT FOR MILLER EMS

FFR. Wow. What can I say. It's given me strength and not just physically, but emotionally and spiritually, which I believe is every bit as important. As a matter of fact, I think you need the emotional and spiritual before you can truly develop the physical. It's given me courage to challenge myself. It's given me a family to encourage. It's challenged me to truly love "me" which I always thought I did but have realized I had/have a lot more insecurities than what I thought. It makes me want to fight these insecurities every day! The whole FFR family including the participants along with the coaching staff are what makes this program a WIN!

Marnie Lee Waller
24 year Veteran Police Officer
Sex Crimes Detective

With seven knee surgeries, a herniated disk in my back, and a torn rotator cuff, my body felt like I'd been put into a paint can shaker set on high for about a decade. After a few months of working out with FFR, my chronic pain is gone, my stress level is low and I'm physically able to do the things I'd given up on doing. I'm happier and healthier than I've been in years.

Sergeant Brandon Watkins
19 year veteran Police Officer
Robbery Unit

I've always worked out and tried to stay "in shape." But as I got older and had kids and my job (excuses), I noticed that when I worked out, my workouts had lost intensity and I had lost motivation. FFR brings that back. You absolutely can't match the quality of an FFR workout. From the drive you get from your teammates to the motivation and techniques from quality coaching. You can't show up here and not get results.

Jerod Lum
Police Officer

Fit First Responders changed the way I view fitness. Before I didn't have motivation to get out and workout. After starting FFR, I lost about 35 lbs. and completely changed my life. This program not only teaches you about your fitness but your personal life. I, along with my fellow first responders, are truly getting FIT FOR DUTY AND FIT FOR LIFE.

Capt. Chris Kundrock, NRP 4672
Emergency Medical Services Authority (EMSA)

FFR to me is a program that slaughtered the Satan/Demons I have been fighting with for years. I lost my dad at an early age, 8 years old, I have been a victim of assaults and domestic abuse growing up after my dad's passing! Now I see my mother struggling with her health and fearing every day I am going to lose my mother! FFR has given me a family in God that I know has my back! God has blessed me with the capability to become Fit for Duty and Fit for Life! This allows me to be better not only for myself, but my family and the public!

CJ Vaughn
Patrol Deputy
Tulsa County Sheriff's Office

I started FFR believing that I was strong mentally, but knowing that I was severely lacking physically. Being a Paramedic and a Reserve Officer, I've always known that fitness was an important aspect to my work. Had someone simply told me about the physical and mental changes I would experience in the program, I would never have believed them. Fast forward 1 year and I'm simply amazed at the progress. I've never been pushed to that mental "wall" on such a regular basis. I'm challenged every day I step in the gym and I know that I have the physical ability to survive and win any encounter I face - either as a Paramedic or an Officer – and have a confidence I didn't always have before. Physically, my job is so much easier. I no longer worry about getting a heavy patient up, I do it right because I can do it.

Shawn Burch
FTO, NRP - EMSA
Reserve Police Officer

Over the past five years, I have struggled with my weight. I have been between 10-25 pounds over what the Army considers my weight should be. I have tried to workout on my own, but the weight has always been a struggle to lose. I knew that my diet was not where it needed to be, but lacked the motivation and desire to change my eating habits. In the last six months, I have been able to meet the Army's standard through FFR's support and encouragement. Having the support and planned workouts at FFR are what keep me motivated to continue striving for my ultimate goal.

Having friends and support not only physically, but spiritually, is amazing. So many of us go through life day in day out without the support or encouragement many of us need. I know that every day I leave FFR that I am physically and mentally strong.

Staff Sargent Adam Ngotngamwong
Oklahoma National Guard supply Sgt

Being a part of this program has been a game changer for me. I feel stronger physically than I have in years. It has helped me focus mentally on things in my life that need improvement and given me motivation and encouragement to make changes. Emotionally, I feel like it's my daily stress reliever. The positive environment created here has carried over into my own life and helped me to become a more positive person.

April Harding
Field Training Police Officer

Have you ever looked in the mirror and wondered how you can be better? A better mom, friend, wife, or Soldier? "Fit First Responders" is my go to guide on how to be my best... not only in fitness, but in my everyday life. It's all about a positive, winning mindset in life and Coach JC's book is a template for all first responders to do just that; a template to be the best version of ourselves.

SSG Lauren N. Olson
RRNCO OKARNG

FFR has given me another way of dealing with stress constructively instead of keeping it inside and just dealing with it. I have been able to improve my diet giving me more energy to be able to deal with the outside stressors. I also have more energy to be able to play with my children. This book will help give guidance to first responders in areas they may not have all of the information in.

Lieutenant Anthony Jones
Department of Veterans Affairs

FIT FIRST RESPONDERS™

BE YOUR BEST PHYSICALLY, MENTALLY, EMOTIONALLY & SPIRITUALLY TO BE FIT FOR DUTY & FIT FOR LIFE.

Coach JC

Johnathan Conneely

WWW.COACHJC.COM

To ALL of the finest, bravest, toughest HEROES,

our first responders. Thank you for your self-sacrificing

commitment to protect and serve the communities

of our great country.

We honor you, recognize you, and thank you for being you.

CONTENTS

Section Five: CREATE THE WINNING MINDSET

MY PRAYER FOR YOU

You were born with a purpose. You have a purpose. I pray for this hero and the person and leader you called them to be. I ask that you anoint every word on every page of this book to become real in their life as they commit to be their best. We believe and pray for their future and for their steps to be ordered by you. Inspire thier heart to make each prayer purposeful, action intentional and words directed. Give them courage to fight and may your holy spirit lead them as they lead and impact so many lives. Bless them now and in the future and look over their entire family and career as a first responder. We thank you that you are working together all things that concern them. Bless them and give them peace, joy and supernatural strength to endure. Move in mighty ways in their life as they commit to be fit for life and be their best. I speak healing right now to their body, heart and mind. I pray your will be done in this heroes life starting today. In Jesus name, Amen.

WIN ALL DAY!

In each chapter there are QR Codes that link to 25 exclusive videos featuring Coach JC coaching you to be FIT FOR LIFE. What does it take for you to be FIT FOR LIFE? In each chapter you will not only read the gameplan but also be provided insightful videos from Coach JC so that you can be empowered and motivated to BE YOUR BEST. You can download a free QR Code reader app onto your phone from your phone's app store. Using your smartphone camera, just scan the QR Code by taking a picture of the code in each chapter of the book, and the video for that chapter will automatically appear in your smartphone browser. You can also type in the link under each QR code and you will be brought directly to that video as well.

FOREWARDS

I am so excited for you; yes, you. What you are about to accomplish in the next 25 weeks will be a tremendous undertaking, radically transforming your mind, body and spirit. Coach JC has developed a manual to help you WIN at LIFE. That's right, a manual to help you WIN at LIFE. I came to Fit First Responders in November of 2015 and I was broken. I was 30 pounds heavier than I am today. I was stressed out over small things in life that I should never have let affect me. My mindset was as weak as my physical body. But that all changed the moment I walked through the doors of our gym and met Coach JC and his incredible coaching staff.

I knew in my heart I was letting my fellow firefighters down because of my physical shape. I was also letting down my community - the same community I swore to protect with my life, the community that was paying me to be in the best shape physically and mentally. They expect an ironman triathlete to be their firefighter and what they were getting at the time was a middle aged, overweight liability. I knew better and had always been in good to great shape over the course of my career, but at the time, I was not taking care of myself.

I was missing the point of why the public was paying me to be a public servant. I had no self-discipline. I had become a chief officer in my organization, but I couldn't even lead myself because of my physical and mental state. That's not what the public expects; they expect the best and I knew in my heart that I was letting them down.

My life transformed once I began my journey with Fit First Responders (FFR). I was not only getting in better shape physically, but my mental game was also coming back. I was motivated again to be the best version of me as well as the best public servant to my community and organization. The positive message and learning that my mindset is really up to me started to change the way I emotionally handled both my personal and professional life.

I have heard and read this old Native American story that says a person has two wolves inside of him. The wolves represent good and evil and whichever wolf you feed, the stronger that wolf becomes. If you're feeding the negative, bad, evil, wolf all the time, what you will get are the negative outputs in your performance and your view on life. However, if you feed the good, positive wolf, your return on investment is a winning mindset that can exponentially change the way you live.

Coach JC has put together a program to help you be successful in all areas of your life and in the next 12 to 25 weeks, if you follow the principles of his program, I promise you'll see positive change in your life. Change will not happen if you don't completely buy into the program. I would encourage you to read each chapter twice and do the work at the end of each chapter. If you commit to these principles and

Coach JC's program, I promise you, you will live a more authentic life than ever before. Plus, you will WIN at LIFE and be the best version of you.

Respectfully,

Chuck French
District Fire Chief
Tulsa Fire Department

If you have ever tried to get into shape, eat better or work on a positive mindset, then you are fully aware of not only the difficulty of accomplishing those things, but also the myriad of schemes that are out there trying to get your attention and money. It is an overwhelming proposition. Or at least it was until now.

FIT FOR LIFE can literally change every aspect of your life. It starts with what you hold in your hands. The 25 chapters of this book will give you a step-by-step playbook to guide you in exactly what you have to do, not only today, but what you must do forever. If you don't believe what I'm saying, then I dare you to open up these pages and discover what will be the beginning of a new life.

It starts with the "4 Pillars" and then outlines a game plan that is easy and progressive to follow. By following one chapter a week, you will build on lessons that will change not only your body, but your mind as well. In just a few weeks, you will see progress that you never thought was possible.

I understand if you are just a little cynical at this point. I was you just a year ago, but very likely much worse. I was losing in life in just about every way you can imagine, but then I started Coach JC's program with week one and I just believed in the process. When your body, mind and even your friends tell you to stop, I promise you that if you just continue, it will all change just like it did for me.

This book and FFR Online brings everything that I did that made my transformation possible, directly to you. This is not a theory or a way to make money. FIT FOR DUTY-FIT FOR LIFE is a proven method to make your life everything that you thought it should be.

I encourage you to just turn the pages and let Coach JC and his words change your definition of "normal" forever.

Travis Yates
Editor in Chief
Law Officer Magazine
www.lawofficer.com

PREFACE

I'll never forget the day in Tulsa, Oklahoma, when the news came across my phone that a local police officer had taken his own life. One of the finest and bravest heroes committed suicide. "WHAT?!" was the first word I recall running through my mind and saying aloud. "WHAT?!"

Then I asked myself, "How?" How does a HERO, the finest and bravest, get to this point?

Sitting there with a heavy heart, I contemplated what was to be said that day when I walked into Fit First Responders and faced over 400 first responders who had just heard the same news as me. I remember it like it was yesterday; "NO! NO! NO!" As I sat in my car outside the FFR training facility, I cried out in pain for this young man and the family he left behind. I cried out with a heavy heart for his friends and colleagues in uniform, many of whom I knew personally and would be interacting with that very day... even in the next few minutes.

The training sessions went on like usual that day; high energy, hard work was put in.... but it was different. The feeling in the facility was just different. You know that feeling when no one knows what to say and time just passes, the job gets done, but there were heavy hearts, there were all kinds of emotions, many of the regulars didn't show up that day and we knew... they were grieving for their brother in blue.

I'll never forget the words spoken by another officer that

day: "I believe that if that officer had been a part of FFR, he would be alive today."

That hit me hard. Guilt ran through my mind and bombarded my soul...Why was he not a part of our FFR program?

That day I made an oath to the over 500 first responders from over 40 agencies in our FFR program. From that day forward, I and my team would do a better job assuring that every first responder, every HERO, would have the opportunity to be a part of FFR.

This police officer who took his own life was not a part of our FFR program. I didn't know him well, though I'd crossed paths with him on a few casual occasions. But I did believe what his fellow officer said, I believe that if that officer had been a part of FFR, he would be alive today.

Just a few weeks later, I had a friend take his own life. I write this book today, not because it's some job for me... this is a calling! I am on a mission...my team is on a mission to fulfill the oath I made that very day. We will do our very best to assure that our nation's HEROES, our first responders, have the opportunity to be FIT FOR DUTY. FIT FOR LIFE.

You say, "Come on, Coach JC! What makes you think the FFR program could have saved his life?" I'll share that answer with you in the next few pages, but first I want you to ask yourself a question...

"Was I THE BEST version of me today?"

Think on that and we will get back to it in a few minutes.

I have been blessed and privileged to work with our nation's finest and bravest in helping them be FIT FOR DUTY... but most importantly, in helping them be FIT FOR LIFE. I have become a student of human nature, learning what makes the finest and bravest, the finest and bravest. Is it the title? Is it the pride of wearing a badge? Is it promoting in rankings?

Many first responders become one of the finest and bravest the day they graduate and walk out of their agency's academy. They are young, ambitious and have a hunger to be the best and fight the good fight. With this fire and this passion to be a great first responder, this fire to save the day, they jump ALL IN and invest everything they have in their profession. They start to sleep and breath it; it starts to become who they are. Then all of a sudden, they wake up one day and wonder, "How did I get here?"

"Being a cop has changed me!"

"I only have to put in a few more years as a firefighter, and then I'm out of here!"

What happened to the fire...the zeal...the "I'm a hero about to save the day" mentality? You look in the mirror one day and don't even recognize that hero any longer. You gave so much to the profession, the team, but you forgot about the MVP. You poured so much in but forgot to get filled back up.

Your body's broken physically...

Your marriage and relationships are dead…

As a parent, you are non-existent…

You are broken, but your pride won't let you show it. "I'm the baddest and toughest…I don't show weakness!"

Your type-A personality doesn't allow you to share this… so you carry on day after day and put the badge on and play the hero role, but deep down inside, you are drowning.

You just know there is more and you desire to be more. You grow bitter, angry and actually build up some resentment towards the job because you feel it robbed you of who you were called to be.

This leads to a lack of self–esteem and low self-worth.

Shifts feel like they are getting longer, you sleep less, poor nutritional habits are your norm now and lack of exercise leads to a sedentary lifestyle.

Your emotions start to control you and you start to act on how you feel. Your low sense of self-worth easily affects other areas of your life. You withdraw from the family and the people closest to you. You just do your job and try to decompress on your weekend or days off so you can once again come back at it next shift. Retirement draws near and the possibility of you becoming a statistic is real. The average mortality rate of our nation's first responders is only 62-64 years of age.

Trying to keep up with the Jones' has hurt you financially. Debt has set in. When you used to be excited to get home after work, you are now going to the bars to wash away the sorrow. Church used to be a Sunday ritual with the family; now it's an Easter and Christmas only event. You are using other things and addictions to mask the real problem.

It has become a cycle.... Now you're in so deep, you don't even see a way out.

How do I know? Because I've been there.

I had a story that I created for myself. I was going to be a collegiate basketball player until I ended up face down in a 600 square foot apartment, contemplating if I was going to go on with life.

We all have that story that we have created for ourselves and our lives. What happens when it's turned upside down and is not going the way we had planned?

I have coached thousands of people who have been there. I have coached thousands of your very own, the finest and bravest who have been there and some who are there even today in life.

YOU ARE A HUMAN BEING! It's normal. The only difference is you see more in a week than the average person sees in their lifetime.

You may be going through it right now in life and every day you are doing the rescuing, but deep down inside, you are the one needing to be rescued. Your story may not be as dramatic as our hero who took his life, but you may just want to be more and achieve more in life.

One thing I know for sure is that as a first responder, you

deserve better than an average life or mediocre life; you deserve THE GREATEST life. You are the finest and bravest and you should live each day to the fullest. You're human; of course you are going to have the normal problems everyone else faces. You are going to go through the trials and tribulations of life, the stresses, the ups and the downs. It's all good! You're not alone!

Your identity is not in who you are as a first responder, it's in who you were created to be. So many times we are fooled into believing that the things that happen to us control our lives, that the events, circumstances and environment we are in have shaped who we are today. This is true if you allow it to be, but I want you to hear me right now - Those things do not make you who you are; their effect is only as strong as your belief in what they mean to you and how you respond to them.

Is it possible to break the cycle?

The answer is, YES!

The answer is for you to BE YOUR BEST! That is why I wrote this book, to provide you with a game plan to be FIT FOR LIFE. When you first saw the book and saw the word FIT on the cover, you probably thought this is all about physical fitness, but being FIT goes way deeper than that, my friend. This is about you being THE BEST version of you and maximizing your God-given talent on this earth.

Back to the powerful question I posed earlier: "Was I the best version of me today?"

Not, "Was I good?"

Not, "Did I survive?"

Not, "Thank God I made it through another day!"

YOU ARE A HERO! You deserve to BE YOUR BEST!

"Was I THE BEST version of me?"

When I made that oath to ensure that every first responder has the opportunity to be a part of FFR, that is what it was about... providing the HEROES of our nation the opportunity to BE THEIR BEST, to WIN in life physically, mentally, emotionally, spiritually, relationally, professionally and financially. In this book, I will not provide you with step by step instructions in the way to train in any of those areas, but I will rather provide you with the game plan to ensure that you can and will WIN in all those areas. Every action originates with a thought. Just like you train your body, you train your mind and that, my friend, is how you become FIT FOR LIFE. That is what FFR does; we are in the business of the personal development of our first responders.

When that hero took his life, I remember meetings being held within departments and agencies with people talking about how to prevent that kind of thing from happening again. My question was different. I asked, "Why did this happen?"

The answer is simple. Many agencies spend a tremendous amount of time developing the first responder, training them in the skills needed to perform their job. I think we would all agree that a large amount of time should be invested into the tactical side, training first responders to be the best at their job. But when are we developing the human being? The MVP?

When's the last time you walked into a squad meeting and were provided a game plan to be THE BEST you in your life outside of the job?

When's the last time you had a huddle with the team at shift change to not only discuss winning on the job but winning in life?

When's the last time an agency spent time providing the skills to our HEROES to help them WIN in their physical body, relationships, spiritual life, mindset and emotions?

You are the finest and bravest. You deserve THE BEST. You are the baddest and toughest but let's not forget, you are HUMAN BEINGS FIRST.

It's not your agency's fault. I don't blame the unions. This is not what they do. This is not their responsibility. They are not in the business of personal development. But people perish for lack of knowledge and this is why FFR was created.

I have been blessed to spend time in squad meetings, shift meetings, at stations, as a coach, friend and just as an observer and I know that FFR is the missing link to creating the WINNING agency. With FFR, you will see sick days decrease, team morale and teamwork improve, healthcare premiums go down, more efficient first responders on the job, but most importantly as an agency, YOU will leave a legacy. With FFR in your agency, you can know that you not only developed great first responders, but great human beings who won in life.

I choose at FFR to make personal development a high priority for our first responders because if you truly want to have the strongest, greatest first responding agency, I know you must build and train up the human being. You eliminate the weakest links by raising the standard of a first responder's personal life, so that they can bring their best to the job. Build up the best human beings and when they are winning in life, it will allow them to truly be their best on the job. How do I know? Because this is real life and in real life, it is impossible to be your best at something when your body is broken and your mind is focused on the stresses of life. As much as you want to leave your baggage at the door, you bring it to the workplace and it effects your performance on the field.

I saw the best cops, the best firefighters, the best medics and national guardsmen on point...but as human beings, many of them were losing in life. They needed a game plan to be on point in the other areas of their life. That game plan could be the difference between life and death. A hero doesn't just wake up one day and take his own life. It's day after day of losing that eventually becomes too much to cope with.

Most agencies have a psychologist on board or at least available for their first responders. I am all about these professionals being in place because many HEROES use them when it hits the fan...but I'm talking about putting in place a solution before the problem escalates. My goal is for FFR to be

PREHAB (prevent it now so we don't have to rehab it later) for our heroes. FFR has become therapy for many first responders in our nation, it has become rehab, it has become family, it has become their go-to in order to help them grow as a human being and WIN in life, and I love that.

You hear it said all the time by first responders, "The goal at the end of the night is to go home to my family." But let me ask, once you get home, then what? Many first responders are bringing their job related issues home and it is affecting their families and life outside the job. What good is it if we have a department filled with HEROES and from the outside it looks like we are winning, but many members of the team are losing in life? Suicides, heart attacks, depression, discouragement, hopelessness, broken marriages, fatherless children, and goals and dreams left on the table are unacceptable for our HEROES.

That is why this book was written - to develop the human beings who are first responders. This book is to provide you with a game plan to WIN in life; to provide agencies with a game plan to help develop the human being parallel to developing the first responder.

What good is it if YOU as a HERO are winning on the street but losing in life? Now is your time! If you want to be more and achieve more in your life - physically, mentally, emotionally, spiritualty, relationally, professionally, financially - then this is the game plan for you.

If you know a first responder, I need your help in getting this game plan in their hands.

Thank you for the opportunity to be your coach and here is to you being FIT FOR LIFE. ALL DAY!

Coach JC

A COUPLE OF FIT FOR LIFE STORIES:

Deputy Chief, Andy Teeter says his department took a leap of faith with FFR and they are glad they did.

When Coach JC first approached the Tulsa Fire Department about Fit for Duty, Fit for Life, I was apprehensive. We get approached by groups all the time that want access to our folks. Many have a self-serving motive. Bar none, our firefighters are the greatest group of competent and caring people you will find anywhere, so naturally we are very protective of who gets their foot in the door and has access to our folks.

We sat down and met with Coach JC and his team. Probably the most striking attributes that they had were their level of enthusiasm and (quite frankly) Coach JC's audaciousness. When I first started hearing what his vision was, I couldn't help but wonder "why?" We heard him out. We ended up giving Coach JC access to our folks, but we made him do the work. He had to go out to our thirty fire stations on three shifts, talk to our folks, and sell this thing.

In the background, while Coach JC was out doing his magic connecting with fire, police, and EMS providers in Tulsa, we got called "downtown" to city hall. The administrations of TFD and TPD sat with the highest ranking members of the city administration and were basically put in a position of defending this thing. There were questions about tax implications and ethics with a City of Tulsa employee winning a truck. They wanted to know about fairness to other city employees, injuries, etc. TFD and TPD took a leap of faith and defended this untested program. In my mind, Coach JC's program wasn't one of the typical coercive programs to reduce injuries or some other knee-jerk program we often see. It was a long term, incremental, far-reaching solution to about ten different deep-seated issues that first responders and first response agencies face every day.

Fast forward to Day 1, 0515 hours. I showed up to FFR with a group of thirty or so firefighters, police officers, and EMTs. My wife, also a firefighter, was leading me along. I'm not workout averse, but over a long period, I had let all the other priorities in life take precedence over taking care of me. I had no idea what was in store, but I knew I needed whatever was about to happen. Coach JC lit us up. The level of enthusiasm was indescribable. I'm pretty sure that most of us were out of our comfort zones that first week. We were appreciated and honored in a way that many of us had never seen. We had to yell out enthusiastically in response to cues. We were asked to walk the turf at the end of every session and connect with someone we didn't know. We had to choose an accountability partner and connect with the entire FFR group on a Facebook page.

It was obvious that this wasn't just a gym. The team we all saw in that first week showed us that this was their life and their passion. There was definitely an underlying, well thought out plan for the program. It was evident that Coach JC and his team had a time-tested methodology. There was something different about these folks, even beyond the level of professionalism, the enthusiasm, and the pain. There was no stopping them. I couldn't put my finger on what was different, but there was something different.

We worked out and we learned about the pillars – focus, food, fitness, family. We gathered at the end of every session and reinforced the pillars. The pillars were a real deal here. We wore blue on Tuesdays to honor the police and red on Fridays to honor military and fire. Soon, Friday sessions had the national anthem before each session. The cops in the group probably picked up on it first. Many police officers I know have had training in picking up on the small clues. I started connecting dots as well. To a person, all of the members of Coach JC's team were unashamedly grounded in their faith, and they had servant's hearts. If anyone hadn't picked up on the faith aspect during the first part of the program, they figured it out pretty quickly when we started praying as a group at the end of every session. Coach JC and his team were infinitely connected with a vast network of folks who were pouring out their love and resources for the first response community. Jim Glover, a prominent Tulsa businessman, probably put it best when he was honoring Coach JC at our FFR Banquet – "You are a fisher of men."

Early on, Coach JC made each group at each session celebrate successes. Very quickly, we saw folks show up claiming they'd been to the doctor and gotten of blood pressure and diabetes medications. That was impactful, but soon the stories of saved marriages and other amazing life changes came flowing in.

We started the program in April of 2015. I had just gotten out of surgery in February for a hiatal hernia that sent me to the hospital. I was in a pretty decent amount of pain from injuries I sustained in 2006. I was taking several medications to make it through each day. When I started attending, I honestly didn't think I would make it through the summer without having back surgery. The back surgery never happened. Now, a year and a half later, I take an anti-inflammatory in the morning and acetaminophen when I need it. Between the program and the special access our members have to Coach JC's preferred chiropractor, my pain dropped to a very manageable level.

I'm not the best example of consistency or weight loss, but I am one of Coach JC's most staunch supporters. I still let work priorities edge me out of showing up at FFR as often as I should. But even with these indiscretions on my part, I have seen amazing results in my family life and in the way I feel each day. I have seen so many of our folks make amazing transformations and experience life changes. But all of these results and the amazing effect they have had on our first responders and military folks are nothing compared to one of our most cherished aspects of the program that probably could have been predicted, but I don't know if we really saw it coming. When you put a bunch of hard-wired folks together who have very high stress jobs and who often have to compete against each other because of the nature of our government, and you make them sweat and bleed all over one another, all of the walls begin to fall down. Cops, firefighters, and medics not only start getting along better than they probably ever have, but they also start lifting each other up and taking selfies together out on the street and posting them on Facebook.

Deputy Chief Andy Teeter
Firefighter

Alexander Peiffer's results at Fit First Responders just get better and better!

I'm Alexander Peiffer, I am 31 years old and a Tulsa Police Officer.

There are so many great things about FFR. The camaraderie among the participants, coaches and all first responders is amazing. The results and the coaching are what keep me coming back. I have lost 18 pounds and my vest now touches on the sides again for full protection. My body comp analysis indicated I had lost 20 pounds of fat alone.

I have been able to really win in my nutrition and in maintaining the 90% compliance rule of FFR. My body fat percentage went from 24% to 17%! I can now keep up with my daughters. The girls come with me to the gym, and my efforts and what they see in me are helping to influence their outlook on challenges. They are adopting the no-quit attitude!

I have a longer fuse, more patience, much higher confidence levels, a better marriage, increased stamina and endurance. I am capable of helping more...I have the strength to just keep going.

Just do it. FFR can only help you as a first responder to BE YOUR BEST. I had amazing results and it's just getting better. Try it and WIN!

Alexander Peiffer
Police Officer

Aaron McGhee misses Fit First Responders on the days he has to work!

I'm Aaron McGhee, I'm 42 years old and I'm an 12-year veteran with the Tulsa Fire Department.

FFR is family. I know now that if I start to lose track, there will be someone there to pick me up. You know that the person next to you is hurting just as bad as you are, so it makes you keep pushing and that in turn makes them keep pushing. The coaches are great. At first it was hard getting used to all the "rah rah," but now I really enjoy it. The coaches know how to keep you motivated.

My results are very encouraging to me. I started the program weighing 253 pounds and I now weigh 236. I haven't been that weight in at least ten years and probably even longer. I am fitting into clothes that have not fit for a long time, and I now need to go get new bunker gear because they are too big!

I miss being at FFR on the days I have to work. I have seen a lot of the other first responders getting slimmer and stronger and more FIT FOR DUTY. That motivates me! I can definitely tell I'm getting stronger. I am happier about myself and am in better shape than I have been in for a long time. I am now more confident about my abilities at work.

I am eating better than ever and am sleeping really well at night. Even on the days when I am really sore from a hard workout, I still feel better than if I was just sitting on the couch doing nothing.

Like Nike says...'Just Do It!' If you think that you don't have the time, find another excuse. We all have the same amount of time in the day and must make time to be FIT. You can make any excuse you want to not go work out... You just need to find an excuse TO GO work out!

Aaron McGhee
Firefighter

4 PILLARS TO BE FIT FOR LIFE

FIT FOR DUTY. FIT FOR LIFE.

⊹	🏃	✗	👥
FOCUS	FITNESS	FOOD	FAMILY

YOU are the Finest!

YOU are the Bravest!

YOU are the Toughest!

YOU are the Baddest!

As a first responder, it's your obligation to be FIT FOR DUTY. You are a warrior and every single day you MUST be ready for battle. In the world we live in, it is absolutely crucial for you to be on your "A-game" at all times when on DUTY. Why? Because your LIFE is on the line.

That is why we created your 4 F's to Be FIT 4 DUTY and our www.FitFirstResponders.com community.

But it doesn't stop there...

At Fit First Responders, we are committed to equipping you to be YOUR BEST - FIT FOR DUTY and FIT FOR LIFE. You deserve to be the best version of YOU that you can be, but many times the stresses of your job can take away from you being your best when you are off duty. The fact that you are taking the time to go through this program tells me that you want to WIN more and be YOUR BEST in life.

As a first responder, every day you witness the power of choice. You know how one decision can radically impact someone's life... for the good or bad. One choice, one decision can change a life forever. Sometimes we make decisions (or fail to make decisions) that, over time, lead us to a place we don't really want to be... to that place where we may not even recognize the person in the mirror anymore. Then we ask ourselves, "How did I get here?"

You are the real HEROES right here in our country and you deserve THE BEST. You deserve to be FIT FOR LIFE! FIT FOR LIFE is about you maximizing your God-given talent on this earth. What good is it if you are great on the job, but you lose in other areas of your life? Sadly, this is a reality for many of our first responding HEROES. That is why this program was created: To provide a game plan so you can WIN in life.

The 4 F's were created to provide you with four pillars so that every single day, you can choose to be YOUR BEST by becoming FIT FOR DUTY and FIT FOR LIFE. Being FIT is about being the best YOU physically, mentally, emotionally, spiritually, professionally and relationally. You will create the right WINS with improvements in your FOCUS, FOOD, FITNESS and FAMILY.

I have been blessed and privileged to start Fit First Responders and www.FitFirstResponders.com, a foundation created to improve the health and work performance of policemen, firemen, National Guard and EMSA workers. As a first responder, you are so important to our communities as you keep us safe, and I am honored to help you WIN more in life.

FOCUS

Being FIT FOR DUTY. FIT FOR LIFE takes the right FOCUS. You focus on what you desire, and what you focus on is what you go and get. It all starts with your mindset. Just like you train your body, you must train your mind. Starting today, shift your focus to what is right in your life and no longer focus on what is wrong. Focus on thinking like a winner, speaking like a winner and acting like a winner, no matter how you may feel at the moment. This 25-week game plan will help you train your mindset so that you can ultimately be FIT FOR LIFE.

FITNESS

As a first responder, you have to be as FIT as you can be. Building the strongest physical, mental, emotional, spiritual and relational you is a must. You must be FIT in all of these areas to WIN in life. I meet firefighters everyday who are losing in their physical body and it's effecting their performance on and off the job. Not you! Not any longer. Today, make the decision to become the most FIT you. It takes a FIT, strong you to be FIT FOR DUTY. FIT FOR LIFE.

We have created the ONLY community for first responders to be FIT FOR DUTY. FIT FOR LIFE, with daily online first responder workouts for all fitness levels and abilities. Get over to www.FitFirstResponders.com and become part of a winning family.

FOOD

With the stresses of your job, it is crucial that you use food for its main purpose, to provide life to your body so that you have the clarity and focus you need to perform at your highest level. I created "Coach JC's 10 Habits to WIN in Your Nutrition" to help you do exactly that. Starting today, make the decision to eat food that will provide life to your body. Being FIT FOR DUTY. FIT FOR LIFE requires a commitment to make good food choices. At www.FitFirstResponders.com , we deliver to you the nutritional coaching, recipes, meal plans and online community so you can WIN in your eating habits.

FAMILY

Every successful team has players who choose to be their best. The best teams become close, like family. They choose to work together to execute a game plan so that they can accomplish one common goal. As a first responder, you are a part of a team. Your department is your team, your family. The other first responders in your city make up your team, your family. It's important that each player is their best and makes the other players on their team their best. Iron sharpens iron and at www. FitFirstResponders.com , we created a community where first responders can build the right relationships to help each other WIN in life.

As of this writing, we have over 500 first responders from over 45 agencies participating with more joining the community each day. You can have anything you want in life when you are surrounded with the right people in the right environment. Starting today, choose to be the best team player you can be and make those on your team their best. Starting today, welcome accountability into your life to make you the best you can be. To be FIT FOR DUTY. FIT FOR LIFE, it takes teamwork within the family. During your 25-week program, you will work as a team to WIN as a team.

TAKE ACTION NOW!

There are two things you need to do right now before you start your FIT FOR LIFE game plan:

1. BECOME A PART OF THE FFR FAMILY.

In the book, I am going to give you a personal development game plan so that you can WIN in life. Online, we have the entire FIT FOR DUTY community game plan. Get over to www. FitFirstResponders.com now and sign up for your free 7-day trial. This is the community built for first responders ONLY.

www.FitFirstResponders.com

2. JOIN OUR FACEBOOK PAGE.

This is a community for first responders. Our professional coaches, team chiropractor, physical therapist, psychologists, dietician, combative team, and many more experts are there to help you WIN. We continually post updates and tips and first responders from all over the country share ideas and network.

Go to facebook.com

Search "FIT FIRST RESPONDERS"

This program was created to insure that you are FIT FOR LIFE. The program is what you make it, so "FIT FOR LIFE" holds whatever meaning you choose to give it. It's about you being YOUR BEST and winning in ALL areas of your life.

Your mindset is a powerful thing, as every action starts with a thought. In this program, the FOCUS pillar and the FAMILY pillar will teach you how to be FIT FOR LIFE by changing your thinking. Think of it as having your very own life coach. I have been blessed to serve as a life coach for some of our nation's top first responders from all different rankings. From my experience in the field, I've developed this program to assure that every HERO out there has the opportunity to WIN in life. This is the ultimate personal development program, life coaching program, mentorship and leadership program all in one, just for first responders.

Over the next 25 weeks, you will learn how to become mentally strong, think big, break through limiting factors, create wins and ultimately be FIT FOR LIFE. You'll be coached to BE

YOUR BEST physically, mentally, emotionally, relationally, professionally, financially and you'll be encouraged to MAXMIZE your God-given talent on this earth. FIT FOR LIFE is about you living the abundant life. It's about discovering your identity, knowing your value and living each day to the fullest with fun and joy as you walk out your purpose.

WHO IS THIS GAME PLAN FOR?

This game plan has been created for the first responder.

*The First Responder** who wants to be better in an area of life (physical, mental, emotional, spiritual, relational, financial, professional).

*The Training Academy** that wants to not only put great first responders on the street, but also develop great human beings as well.

*The Chief** who wants his team, his department to create unity and build team camaraderie.

*The Leadership (Captain, Sergeant, Corporal, etc...)** who wants to have a game plan for the team to follow to raise the culture of the department, setting higher standards and investing in the lives of their first responders.

HOW DOES THIS PROGRAM WORK?

There are three ways you can effectively implement the FIT FOR LIFE For First Responders program:

Execute one lesson every day for 25 consecutive days.

Execute two lessons a week for a 12-week game plan.

Make it a 25-week game plan by implementing just one lesson each week.

The third option is how I recommend implementing the program and many departments and agencies have utilized this format very successfully with their teams. Kick off each week with 15-30 minutes of team huddle before shift starts to go over that week's lesson. Then the other days of the week, hold 15-minute breakout sessions as a team to discuss the lesson and share WINS throughout the week. This gives you a 25-week personal development game plan as you work through and on one lesson per week.

The goal is for you to execute the game plan, adopting these principles as part of who you are as a first responder, a team player and most importantly, as an individual person. These are principles that you will continue to execute, refine and utilize in your journey to be FIT FOR LIFE. This program was created as a game plan that you can keep with you at all times and continue to use, just like any other training tool, as you continue to grow and achieve greatness as a first responder and in life.

For you to be FIT FOR LIFE, you must put the principles into action. The Daily Action Steps must be a part of your training! Retention without implementation is useless, my friend. Find ways to put what you've learned into action in your personal and professional life. Just like you train your body day in and day out, you now have the right game plan to train your mind. Develop the right rituals and habits now so that they become part of your subconscious mind and you can pull on them when needed. By being honest with yourself and taking massive action each day, you will WIN.

The Winning Confession is your time to speak truth! With each lesson, you are given a Winning Confession. Faith comes by hearing and this is your time to speak into your life those things that you desire. It is during this time that you call those things that are not into existence. Some people call this positive affirmation and have experienced great success using this tool. Your Winning Confession is a lot more than just speaking positive stuff and hoping it will come to pass each day. It's about you starting to THINK, ACT, and FEEL as if you're already there! There are three things that you need to do immediately when it comes to your Winning Confession.

You need to SEE IT! SAY IT! SEE IT!

You will SEE IT (the confession) on paper, you will SAY IT like you mean it, then you will SEE IT as accomplished, even though it may not reflect where you currently are. Winning Confessions are powerful, as they build up your faith and inspire creative ways for you to make it happen. You will master Winning Confessions in Lesson 5, "I CAN'T HEAR YOU."

This program will change the way you **THINK (YOUR**

MINDSET), which will create the right **ATTITUDE** on how you look at your life, so that you can execute the proper **ACTIONS** to get the **RESULTS** that you desire and deserve so you can ultimately live the **LIFE** that you were born to live.

Though it may seem strange, we're going to come at the game plan in reverse. The first thing we will do is determine the **LIFE** you desire to live. We can then define the **RESULTS** you need to get to live that life, the **ACTIONS** you must take to achieve those results, the **ATTITUDE** you must choose to exhibit each day and the **MINDSET** you must adhere to if you are going to **WIN**.

WHAT TIME IS IT?

It is time to HONOR
those that deserve to be honored.

It is time to RECOGNIZE
those that deserve to be recognized.

The FINEST! The BRAVEST!

The TOUGHEST!

The BADDEST!

Law Enforcement!

Firefighters!

Medics!

National Guard!

The First Responders of our Nation.

The REAL HEROES of The United States of America.

NOW is YOUR time to be FIT FOR DUTY.

FIT FOR LIFE.

SECTION ONE: BUILD THE **LIFE** YOU DESERVE

CHAPTER ONE

WILL THE REAL YOU PLEASE STAND UP?

"I cannot trust a man to control others
who cannot control himself."

Robert E. Lee

FFROnline.TV/Lesson-1

Will the real Slim Shady please stand up? I used to love that jam by Eminem and today I ask you that same question... Will the REAL you please stand up?

Who are you? STOP! Think about that for a second. What is your answer when someone asks you, "Who are you?"

So many times in life, we allow what we do to define who we are. "I am a mom." "I am a dad." "I am a firefighter." "I am a police officer." That's what you do...not who you are.

What you do is not who you are. **Your identity is not in what you do.**

Your identity is also not defined by your past. So many times, we allow what happened to us in the past to define who we are. Past failures and mistakes don't define you. It doesn't matter what your parents, a teacher, society, or the media told you; it doesn't matter what happen to you as a kid; that's not who you are. That situation, circumstance, or trial does not define you.

It's not who you think you are that holds you back in life, it's who you think you're not.

So let me start by telling you who you're not...

You are not average.

You are not mediocre.

You are not a loser.

You are not an addict.

You no longer walk in fear.

No more guilt.

No more shame.

You are not a victim.

How you may feel at the moment does not define you.

Your worry and fear is not that you are incompetent, incapable or afraid to fail...your deepest fear is that you are powerful, strong and valuable beyond what you can even imagine and see at the moment.

You were born with a purpose. You were born to WIN. You were born to be your best.

You were bought with a price.

You were born a WINNER.

You were born a champion.

You are a child of God.

Your playing small does nothing for the people you love, nothing for your agency and nothing for the world around you. There is nothing special about you shrinking so that other people won't see your flaws or insecurities. We all have them... who cares?!

Today is your day to step into greatness. Today is your day to define who you are.

You are valuable. You are talented. You deserve it. You are worth it. You are more than a conqueror.

Every successful business has a brand. What's your personal brand? What are you about? What do you stand for? Only when you truly discover who you are will you become the best first responder, the best version of you. Once you discover your value, that is when you will ultimately become FIT FOR LIFE.

What are your core values? Dig deep and let's pull out WHO you are at the core. Don't think about how you feel at the moment, but rather who you know you are deep down inside. Who is that person you want to re-awaken on the inside so the world can see?

What words define you? Truthful, honest, team player, positive, professional, integrity, joyful, compassionate, strong, hard-working, disciplined, family, life balance, health, God, faith, dependable, determined, respect, intense, passionate, kind, leader, beautiful. What words would you choose?

Be FIT FOR LIFE by defining WHO YOU ARE. Create your three I AM statements. Your I AM statements reflect who you are and what you stand for.

TAKE ACTION:

I AM _____

I AM _____

I AM _____

WINNING CONFESSION:

Today is my day.

No one will get in my way of me being the best version of me.

I am here on purpose. I have a purpose.

I am strong. I am passionate.

I am powerful. I am unstoppable. I am a winner.

I am fearless. I choose faith.

I AM FIT FOR DUTY. I AM FIT FOR LIFE.

FIT FOR LIFE STORY:

Jennie says Fit First Responders has blessed her in so many ways.

I began my journey in FFR feeling blessed with an opportunity to better myself. In the beginning, my goal was to lose weight and gain strength and conditioning. In reality, this program has blessed me on so many more levels including in **my marriage, my parenting skills, not to mention my physical and emotional state.** My spirit has also been blessed by the coaches and fellow FFR family. The entire program has helped me to Step It Up in Life. I am more confident with myself and like the person I see looking back at me in the mirror, both inside and out!

In the beginning, I was mentally depressed about my roles as a wife and mother of two beautiful daughters. I had checked out of life. I was literally functioning day by day. FFR gave me a reason to get up and focus on myself, a task I have never done. This seemed very selfish at first but it became apparent to me that to be the best wife, mother and firefighter, I had to take time to get healthy mentally, physically and spiritually.

I began to follow the coaches' advice and put it into action. I began to see changes almost instantly and so did family and co-workers. This made me push myself even harder. I developed a bone spur on my right heel partway through the program, but I was encouraged to stay the course and finish. I had to modify a few things along the way, but it has been well worth it for the results I have obtained. Like Coach JC says, "If you want something you've never had, you have to do something you've never done." This was the mindset that kept me pushing myself. In just 25 weeks, I lost a total of 14 pounds, 8.5% body fat and 25 inches and gained muscle to top it all off. I also began to feel like my life was worth something. I AM FIT FOR DUTY. I AM FIT FOR LIFE.

Jennie Teeter

Firefighter

CHAPTER TWO

GET WHAT YOU CAME FOR

"Leadership is a potent combination of
strategy and character. But if you must
be without one, be without strategy."

FFROnline.TV/Lesson-2

Norman Schwarzkopf

What is it that you really want? If you don't know what you want, you will never get it! It all starts right here my friend, with desire. You must want it! You must have a desire to achieve and a desire to succeed!

"Get what you came for!" This is a line that first responders hear from me all the time. But for you to get what you came for, you have to know what it is you came for.

What is that thing that you have wished for or hoped for; that thing that you may have been dreaming about since you were a kid? Maybe it's to be a captain, earn that ranking of chief one day, be an All-American dad, have an AMAZIING marriage, be an entrepreneur, or maybe even retire one day with successful hobbies.

If you don't know what you want, you'll never get it! This is one of the most important questions you can ask yourself. This is where it all starts. What is the LIFE you want to live? The big picture, the thing you dream of, your ultimate goal - what does that look like to you? We all have those things we want to get or achieve, but so many times we stop short of refining it to know EXACTLY what it is. You have to be specific about it. You have to be vivid in your description of it. If you don't know where you want to go, you'll never get there. This is so important because **WHAT YOU DESIRE IS WHERE YOUR FOCUS WILL GO!** Once you know what it is that you desire, you must place a timeline on achieving or obtaining it. When will you accomplish this desire?

Success starts with DESIRE! Most first responders are afraid to put their WHAT out there because they don't want to set themselves up for failure. It is your "WHAT" that will determine where you put your focus and the minute you decide to focus on something, that is the moment you give it meaning in life. That meaning will produce the necessary emotions that create the action to help you obtain your WHAT. Your WHAT will drive you in becoming FIT FOR LIFE.

You have got to be real about your WHAT; be specific about it and put it out there. Michael Jordan was never unclear about his WHAT. When asked about his WHAT, his response was always the same. He played to be THE GREATEST player to ever play the game.

In the pursuit of being FIT FOR LIFE, GET WHAT YOU CAME FOR by defining your WHAT.

TAKE ACTION:

Life Goal Assessment

Name: _____

Today's Date: _____

*BE AS SPECIFIC AS POSSIBLE WHILE ANSWERING THE FOLLOWING QUESTIONS

1. WHAT I want to accomplish in my LIFE:

(These are my outcome goals for the next 25 weeks while committing to the FIT FIRST RESPONDERS Program. (Physically, mentally, emotionally, relationally, professionally, financially, etc...Be specific and vivid)

2. WHY I want to accomplish my goals:

These goals are very important to me because...

3. I will do just about anything except this:
What things am I willing to sacrifice and what habits do I need to break to be FIT FOR LIFE.

4. When I reach these LIFE goals what I will get and how I will feel:

5. My past record of attaining my desired LIFE goals has been.

WINNING CONFESSION:

I WILL BE FIT FOR LIFE and WIN as a FIRST RESPOND-ER and WIN in LIFE. I WILL achieve my greatest potential as the HERO I am and I WILL succeed in LIFE! I am a WINNER! I AM FIT FOR LIFE!

FIT FOR LIFE STORY:

Denise Henry says Fit First Responders is her home and her family!

My name is Denise Henry, I am 16-year veteran police officer, I am a sergeant at Creek Nation Lighthorse Police Department, and I am also an OG from the very first FFR competition in April 2015.

When I started the 25-week challenge, I weighed 190 pounds and at 5 feet 2 inches tall, that meant I was about 50 pounds over my weight limit. I was unhealthy, borderline diabetic, depressed, tired all the time and failing in life. Due to the fact that I was tired and feeling heavy, doing my job was difficult. Getting in and out of the car was a struggle and chasing after a suspect was nowhere at all in my thoughts or capabilities. The first FFR workout was stressful just because of the unknown. I was uneasy about working out because I was unfamiliar with the gym and weights. I also did not know anyone there and being out of shape and in my forties, I felt inferior. I worried I wouldn't be up to par with everyone else and worried about completing even one workout, much less three workouts a week for 25 weeks. But after the first workout, all my stress and worry was replaced with excitement, encouragement and relief that I could do this.

FFR is my home and it is my family. Everyone in this program feels that way. The atmosphere in our FFR family is always comforting to me, regardless of struggles I am going through and obstacles I'm facing on the job or in my personal life. The coaches and the other family members are always there to help you WIN. It's like having over 400 new best friends who do the same job and are facing the same problems, who now look after you and have your back. The coaches are like having your own personal doctor, personal trainer, personal therapist, personal nutritionist, and personal life coach. There's not one thing in life that somebody there hasn't experienced and overcome. **It's my family forever now!**

I lost 25 pounds, but for me, that is not the most important part. I have gained strength and muscle and am in better shape than when I was in my twenties. **For me, the healthy habits I have learned are the most important part.** I eat for nutrition instead of for comfort now. The nutrition is not a diet. People fail on diets. FFR teaches you 10 healthy habits that you follow every day. The nutrition is something everyone can follow every day in their life for the rest of their life. It doesn't matter whether you're cooking or going to McDonald's, you can eat healthy and you can even enjoy not-so-healthy things if you follow the ten habits. We all have our things we love to eat, but we earn them in the gym.

I have more energy and am more focused in everyday life. I am definitely happier and feel better because I am healthier than I have ever been. FFR has helped me become more confident and focused at everything I do and because of that, I am a better employee and a better leader. I have been promoted twice at my agency since joining FFR and now serve as the only female sergeant in my department. I am a better mother, daughter and friend because I'm more focused on my family and my friendships and the important things in life. It's impossible to be in our FFR family without feeling all the positive vibes and love rubbing off on you. I walk around after completing my workout feeling better about life and wanting to be a better person.

These are not just people you see at FFR...they are your family, the ones you may be on a scene with later that night, maybe the ones who will save YOU one day. We are all family on the same team with the same mission and that is the feeling you will have from the first day you join our FFR family and for the rest of your life. **It's my family and it's open to any HERO looking for that kind of support and encouragement.**

Sergeant Denise Henry

Creek Nation Lighthorse Police Department

CHAPTER THREE

WHAT'S MY "WHY"

"You must have dreams and goals
if you are ever going to achieve
anything in this world."

FFROnline.TV/Lesson-3

Lou Holtz

Now that you have defined your I AM's and your WHAT, you need to ask yourself, "WHY?"

When I'm coaching one of our nation's HEROES (that is you), immediately after discovering their WHAT, my next question is always, "WHY?" That's the question I have for you now: WHY do you want your WHAT? WHY do you do what you do? WHY do you want to be chief, have a great marriage, lose the weight, get out of debt, or whatever it is you have as your goal?

I remember it like it was yesterday, I asked this exact question to a first responder I am blessed to train who told me he wanted to get promoted to the next ranking in his agency while taking his side business to the next level. He said, "I have watched my wife work a job so that we could support our family. It has always been my dream to allow my wife to be a stay at home mom, and I believe this will provide her with an opportunity to only work if she wants to."

Man! Is that not a powerful WHY? This HERO had a purpose, a burning desire to accomplish his goal. I get goosebumps thinking about it! I am excited to say that we turned his want into an "I WILL" and he did exactly what he said he would. He was promoted and is now able to allow his wife to be a stay at home mom!

WHY do you want that thing that you want? Determining your WHY is absolutely crucial for you to be FIT FOR LIFE. Your WHY is your purpose: the burning desire that drives you toward your WHAT. Your WHY is the reason you will do what you do, day in and day out, to be YOUR BEST and WIN IN LIFE.

Your WHY will drive you with a burning passion, keeping you motivated to make your dream - your desire - a reality. This is the reason you do what you do, the thing you will stay focused on: The End Result!

For you to truly WIN, you must know your reason WHY. What makes you tick? This is more than your goals; it's your need, your target. It's that thing that pulls on you so strong, you have got to keep going, no matter what. It's your drive, your juice, that thing that lights you on fire (no pun intended, firefighters). Think of it like the fire you had deep inside when you graduated the academy.

I want you to hear me. Your follow through in doing what you need to do to be FIT FOR LIFE comes down to your emotional intensity, which is why your vision has got to be compelling enough to drive you. When your WHY is strong, your emotional intensity will be strong. Every action you take originates with a thought and once your emotional intensity is on point, each and every action you take will rise to that level.

Become FIT FOR LIFE today by defining your WHY.

TAKE ACTION:

Why do I really want this? (Be specific. Be vivid.)

How badly do I want/need this?

What am I willing to do to get it?

What am I not willing to do?

WINNING CONFESSION:

I have been created with a purpose! I am not moved by what I feel or by my circumstances. I WILL take purposeful action to get what I desire. I WILL BE FIT FOR DUTY. I WILL BE FIT FOR LIFE! I am a WINNER.

FIT FOR LIFE STORY:

Heather Greenwood Says Fit First Responders Is the Best Thing Ever!!!

I'm Heather Greenwood, I'm 42 years old and I'm a Tulsa Firefighter/Paramedic.

FFR is the best thing ever! Having the support and encouragement from everyone in my FFR family is awesome. The results are great too. The FFR program gives me my daily dose of adrenaline, motivation, support, and camaraderie with my new friends and family and daily morning prayer. If I don't get it in, I feel like I am just not myself that day. I love to see how much I have improved and continue to improve... mentally, physically, and spiritually.

I love how I have been pushed beyond what I thought my limits were. I am constantly encouraged to be better and do more, which results in me surpassing what I thought I could do. I have lost 16 pounds, seven inches in the waist, 17 pounds of Body Fat Mass, and 67.2% body fat. Seeing my before and after pictures motivated me even more because I don't ever want to go back to the before picture!

I am always in a better frame of mind after I complete my daily FFR game plan. **I have a much more positive attitude on life.** FFR has helped me get back on track. It has improved my eating habits, taught me a lot about nutrition, taught me proper lifting techniques and taught me that I can do way more than I ever thought I could. I have much more stamina now in my workday and outside of work. I am more energetic in life and enjoy doing more things, when before I was just too tired and short of breath. I sleep better. I eat better. I have a more positive attitude toward everyone and toward the things in my life.

FFR has brought me closer to other agencies that I normally would not have the opportunity to encounter. I have met a lot of great people and love them all. **I HIGHLY recommend FFR. It's the best thing ever!!!!!!**

Heather Greenwood

Firefighter

CHAPTER FOUR

WHAT'S MY GAME PLAN?

"You can go by chance and hope to win or you can create, train, and execute a game plan to win."

FFROnline.TV/Lesson-4

Coach JC

Do you have a game plan? All successful people have a plan of action! What's yours? What's your game plan that you will execute to get you to where you need/want to be as a first responder and in life? You have part of your game plan in your hands right now – this book. We will now create your WINNING CONFESSION so that you can get what you desire and deserve.

Your WINNING CONFESSION consists of your three I AM statements, your I WILL statement and your purpose or your WHY, that we created in the Take Action steps in the first three chapters.

Thinking about what you've written in your Take Action steps, I now want you to put together your own professional game plan, specific to that thing you desire as a professional. For example, if you want to be a captain or chief, what are the components necessary for you to become that great leader in your agency? What are you going to do to work on your skill, to develop leadership skills, to perfect your first responder tactics, and so on?

"Never give an order that can't be obeyed."

General Douglas MacArthur

Now, develop your personal game plan. This should be a concrete action plan detailing the necessary components you will utilize to get what you want in your personal life. You will need to have a game plan for each of the key areas you desire to be FIT in - physical, mental, emotional, spiritual, professional, relational and financial.

I want you to think back to the answers you gave in chapter 2 as you detailed your WHAT. Hear me as I say this:

YOU DESERVE IT! YOU DESERVE IT! YOU DESERVE IT!

Today, to be FIT FOR LIFE, you will create your WINNING CONFESSION and professional and personal game plan.

TAKE ACTION:

My WINNING CONFESSION.

I AM_____

I AM_____

I AM_____

I WILL_____

MY WHY IS_____

My Professional Game Plan Is...

My Personal Game Plan Is...

WINNING CONFESSION:

I AM A PERSISTENT AND DILIGENT HERO. I will work hard each and every day so that I will be THE BEST version of me. I WILL BE FIT FOR DUTY. I WILL BE FIT FOR LIFE! I DESEREVE IT! I am a WINNER!

FIT FOR LIFE STORY:

Dakota Crase finds so much support in his Fit First Responder Family!

I'm Dakota Crase, I am 28 years old and I'm a Tulsa County Sherriff's Deputy.

FFR has become my family and that's what keeps me coming back. The FFR family and community depends on each of us, not only in the gym but also on the streets. **Being physically and mentally fit makes facing the day-to-day stress and challenges that much easier.**

I have experienced a lot of great results both physically and mentally. I have lost inches and gained muscle and strength. I've also experienced other changes in my life. I've dipped Copenhagen Long Cut since I was 15. Knowing all the hard work I was putting in at FFR to improve myself, I now saw tobacco and alcohol use as counter-productive. One day during FFR, the urge to dip was gone. **I've never picked it up since.**

The coaches and team at FFR have really challenge me, not only in the gym, but also in life and in my family life. I've become a better person in general because of implementing the four pillars into my daily life.

A little advice for someone considering starting FFR: It's going to hurt. Life is tough at times. You're going to be uncomfortable, and at some point you're going to hit a wall. At FFR, you never hit that wall alone. We have so much support in this family!!!

Deputy Dakota Crase
County Sheriff

CHAPTER FIVE

I CAN'T HEAR YOU!

"All our dreams can come true if we
have the courage to pursue them."

Walt Disney

FFROnline.TV/Lesson-5

This is always a fun and difficult step for the finest and bravest to do. In chapter one, we defined WHO YOU ARE. In chapter two, we identified your WHAT. In chapter three, we determined your WHY. We then put all of that together to create your personal WINNING CONFESSION and game plan that will help you WIN. Now it's time to use it, baby!

You will now take your WINNING CONFESSION and speak it into existence. That's right! You will say it and call those things that are not as if they are. Let me start by saying that I don't believe you can just repeatedly say that you want something and it will happen. I am talking about speaking with a confidence and a belief. This is FAITH. This is believing without a doubt that those things you are speaking and taking action on will come to pass.

Faith comes by hearing and that is why in this book, in each chapter, I provide you with a Winning Confession... to build up that faith. **Faith is not a feeling; faith is a choice.** Faith is believing when others doubt. Faith is focusing on what is unseen in the natural at the moment. Faith is not being moved by what you see or by your current circumstances. Faith is not doing nothing; faith is doing something.

Faith comes by hearing! When you say something over and over again, you will subconsciously find ways to make yourself get to that place. You will start to believe that it is already a reality; therefore, you'll do what's necessary to make it happen. There is tremendous power in your words, my friend. But be careful; this can also work against you if you allow it to. If you keep saying negative things, you won't make any effort, and you will eventually quit because your subconscious mind will have accepted that you will never achieve your goals.

There will be people who will speak against you accomplishing your goal, people who do not want you to succeed, and people who will doubt that you can do what you say you can. Haters will be haters. The way to counteract this negativity is for you to speak what you desire into existence. When you speak against this negativity, you are releasing your confidence, and you are exposing yourself to positive energy.

You will never be FIT FOR LIFE if you are negative and always speaking depressing and doubtful things. When you constantly speak negativity, it makes you unpleasant to be around and very unhappy. Who wants to be around those kinds of people?

I am a big action guy. You can feel confident speaking out your WINNING CONFESSION because you are putting action behind the words! Here is the cool thing: Within one week of speaking your WINNING CONFESSION into existence, you will notice considerable improvement in how you feel about yourself as you build your faith and get closer to reaching your goals.

I CAN'T HEAR YOU! I want you to not just speak your confession, but SPEAK IT WITH AUTHORITY. Say it like you mean it. Use the tone and pitch in your voice and even the non-verbal communication of your body language to express what you really want. Visualize what you want and then speak it and start to see that very thing that you are speaking come to pass! That is how you build faith and OWN THE MOMENT, baby!

There's POWER in your words! Today you will become the greatest salesperson in your life and sell yourself on the reality that ALL THINGS are possible. Today you will become your best coach, your best preacher, you will build your faith and call those things that are not as if they are. You will build your belief, which then will drive your behavior and your behavior will dictate your performance. Change your belief…Change your life!

Today, to be FIT FOR LIFE, you will build your faith.

"FAITH is the substance of things hoped
for, the evidence of things not seen."

Hebrews 11:1, King James Version

TAKE ACTION:

Take your three I AM's, your I WILL, and your WHY and put them into one paragraph. This is your personal WINNING CONFESSION, developed in chapter 4. Now you will SEE IT, SAY IT, SEE IT.

SEE IT – I want for you to write down your WINNING CONFESSION or type it up and place it in three places you see most often throughout the day. I want it to be in front of you throughout the day. Write the vision and make it plain so that you may run with it (Habakkuk 2:2). SEE IT.

SAY IT – I want for you to commit to SAY IT (your WINNING CONFESSION) at least three times a day. When you say it, I want for you to say it out loud. Say it like you mean it. Say it with authority. Utilize the pitch and tone of your voice and non-verbal communication like fist pumping, jumping and clapping. Put emotion behind it. I CAN'T HEAR YOU!

SEE IT – When you say the words of your WINNING CONFESSION, I want you to SEE IT – imagine it and see yourself already there. Get a vision of you already walking out that WINNING CONFESSION. When you say it, I want you to THINK, SPEAK and ACT like you already have it. SEE yourself hitting on all cylinders, winning in life, FIT FOR LIFE physically, mentally, emotionally, spiritually, relationally, financially, and professionally.

WINNING CONFESSION:

Use your personal WINNING CONFESSION and SEE IT! SAY IT! SEE IT!

"I CAN'T HEAR YOU!"

FIT FOR LIFE STORY:

Chief Belk says, "I feel better physically and mentally as well, thanks to Fit First Responders."

I'm Stacy Belk, I'm 49 years old, and I serve as an Assistant Chief for the Tulsa Fire Department.

Fit First Responders has changed my life on a variety of different levels. The program is unlike any other I have ever seen. My favorite aspect of FFR is the spirit of enthusiasm and the effort the coaches put into their jobs to get our first responders in shape. This team and the coaches have a genuine interest in me and make the game plan for being FIT FOR DUTY. FIT FOR LIFE enjoyable. Their passion is not only for my physical wellbeing, but my spiritual wellbeing as well.

Coach JC and his team of coaches, in my opinion, are real, in that they practice what they preach and have a passion for training and teaching first responders.

The atmosphere at FFR that they have created is amazing... it is impossible to lose in this environment. This atmosphere includes opportunities to meet new people, enjoy quality workouts and receive training from quality coaches with genuine caring attitudes. The coaches and fellow participants at FFR push you to be your best and at the same time, they understand that people are at different levels of fitness and capabilities not only in their workout, but also in life. This is the only program I am aware of that has a two-fold purpose: the physical and the spiritual.

I am down 12 pounds and know I've lost some inches. I feel better and have more energy to do things. I am wearing clothes that I have not been able to wear for years. My blood pressure has gone down, and my eating habits have changed for the good.

The best part of the program for me is that when I arrive to work out and I walk through the doors, I am able to leave all my stress, all my worries from my job and life in general outside and focus on what is going on for the next hour. **I use this program as a stress relief valve.** I look forward to going and working out and when I have to miss, I feel bad not only physically but mentally as well. The spiritual/mental part of the program has changed me in ways that I really can't explain, but I can tell you I have a better relationship with my wife, my kids, and my coworkers since starting this program.

FFR has provided me with new friends and basically, a third family. The workouts are great and have helped me physically and in even bigger way, helped me emotionally. The positive attitudes of the coaches and those who are a part of FFR have made an impact that my family has noticed at home.

If you are thinking of trying to become healthier and want

to be FIT FOR LIFE, then this is the place for you. **This is, by far, the best atmosphere that I have ever been associated with. Once you try it, you will be hooked.**

Chief Stacy Belk
Firefighter

SECTION TWO: THE **RESULTS** YOU WILL CREATE

CHAPTER SIX

WIN THE DAY

"Some people want it to happen, some wish it would happen, others make it happen."

FFROnline.TV/Lesson-6

Michael Jordan

Now that you have developed your game plan, it's time to WIN THE DAY, baby!

WIN THE DAY! In the last five chapters, you should have created your game plan so that you can be FIT FOR LIFE. Now let's talk about the daily action steps you'll take to execute your game plan. **What is that one, simple, disciplined thing that you will do each and every day to get where you need to be?** This is called the Law of WINNING, baby.

86,400! 86,400!! 86,400 opportunities every single day to BE YOUR BEST. 86,400 opportunities every day to WIN. There are 86,400 seconds in everyday, 1440 minutes each day...24 hours today for you to WIN. WIN the day by winning the seconds and minutes in knowing that you will never get these opportunities back. Time can work for you or against you, depending on whether you make the most of your time or waste it. On the road to success, this is the step where most people fail. Most first responders desire to be more and achieve more, they know what they want, but very few have daily actions that line up with what they truly desire.

This is where we break up your game plan into daily action steps. Only by following those daily action steps will you execute the game plan to get what it is you truly desire. You have to be very specific as you detail your action steps. For example, if you are an aspiring professional first responder and part of your game plan is to train to be in the best physical shape possible, your game plan better include being a part of FFRONLINE.tv. Your daily action step will be something like, "I will train with my coaches at 5:30 A.M., Monday through Friday at FFRONLINE.tv. at my house in the garage." This action step answers the What, When, Where, and How questions. Be as specific as possible by listing exact times, locations, and step-by step approaches that you will take to get it done. Compiling a written itinerary of what, when, where, and how you will do each daily component will transform you into YOUR BEST and ultimately make you FIT FOR LIFE.

> "If you want be something you've never been or have something you've never had, you better choose to do something every day that you have never done."
>
> Coach JC

Willie Mays once said, "In order to excel, you must be completely dedicated to your chosen sport. You must also be prepared to work hard and be willing to accept constructive criticism. Without a total 100 percent dedication, you won't be able to do this."

Each day before you lay your head on the pillow you should ask yourself, "Did I win the day today?" The Law of WINNING is all about DEDICATION and COMMITMENT, my friend. It's about self-accountability and self constructive criticism. Mentally tough human beings direct their time and focus on what is important to them in chasing their dreams and goals.

Today to be FIT FOR LIFE, you will WIN THE DAY by implementing the Law of WINNING.

TAKE ACTION:

List EVERY area you want to be FIT FOR LIFE in, then consider your game plan. List the daily action step that you will take to execute the game plan. (Be specific -What, When, Where, How)

Example:
Physical Body
I WILL lose 30 pounds and pass my PA test by_____.
My game plan is FFRONLINE.tv.
My Daily Action Step is

What: FFRONLINE.tv
How: Login from my computer and complete the
WINNING game plan of the day.
When: I will do this at 5:30 A.M. on Monday, Wednesday
and Friday each week.
Where: I will do this at my house in the garage.

WINNING CONFESSION:

I am a go-getter. I am focused on what I want and determined to go get it. I do not go by how I feel, as emotions don't control who I am and what I do. I will take action today. I WILL WIN THE DAY! I am FIT FOR LIFE.

FIT FOR LIFE STORY:

Bobby Zigmont is in the best shape of his life at age 41!

I'm Bobby Zigmont, I'm 41 years old and I'm a Police Officer with the Bixby Police Department, currently assigned to Bixby Public Schools as a School Resource Officer.

FFR has changed my life for the better. I love the very motivating coaching staff, the connection and networking with all the first responders from all the surrounding agencies, and the amazing program that actually has proven results!

The excitement, energy and motivation I get from training with fellow first responders and the amazing transformation I've seen in my body and health keeps me coming back. I have lost over 20 pounds and have blasted through previous personal records on all my lifts. I have stamina and endurance I haven't experienced in years. I am in the best shape of my life at age 41!

FFR has improved my eating habits and changed how I view nutrition. FFR has also improved my focus on what's important to me - my wife and daughter - and has made me more committed to being the best husband and father to them. It has also made me more focused on serving my community by being the best police officer, which is what the citizens deserve. FFR has brought me closer to other police officers, fire fighters, and paramedics I never thought I'd have a friendship with. FFR has given me a renewed excitement to stay fit and be the best I can possibly be.

FFR will ABSOLUTELY give you results, if you bring a desire to be healthier and stronger and the determination to work for what you want the most. With your willingness, the coaches and fellow FFR Warriors will fight alongside you to get you to those results!

Bobby Zigmont
Police Officer

CHAPTER SEVEN

GET BACK IN THE GAME

"Do it even when you don't feel like
doing it and do it over and over again
until you feel motivated to do it."

FFROnline.TV/Lesson-7

Coach JC

JUST DO IT! Nike said it best, baby! You have to do it even when you don't feel like doing it. You are a person who MAKES things happen and starting today, you are back in the game! You're back in the game of life, back in the game of being your BEST.

"Life is 10% what happens to you and
90% how you choose to respond to it."

Charles Swindoll

You have learned over the last few chapters how to create the WINNING mindset so that you can BE YOUR BEST and ultimately be FIT FOR LIFE. Now it's time to JUST DO IT!

"Nothing in life has meaning except
the meaning you give it!"

Tony Robbins

That is powerful! Think about that for a second. With everything that goes on in life...the ups and the downs... the only meaning it will ever have is the meaning you choose to give it! Your health. Your happiness. Your marriage. Your job. What you get out of it all comes down to the meaning that you choose to give it. Many of us have been defeated in these areas, so they now mean little to nothing to us. Because of this, many of us are not even in the game. No matter the failures and setbacks you've experienced, it's not too late. **Today is your day to GET BACK IN THE GAME!**

Today is your day to commit to get back in the game... physically, mentally, emotionally, spiritually, financially, professionally and in your relationships. You are in control and starting today, you will only focus on what you can control. Focusing on the things beyond your control just steals your emotional space and drains you, pulling you out of the game. FIT FOR LIFE is about maximizing your God-given talent on this earth and living the abundant life...a life of joy and happiness so that you can WIN and then help others WIN in life.

I get it, some of you have been through hell and you aren't even on the sidelines anymore. You're in the locker room or even just watching the game on the big screen at the station on Sunday. The reality is, some of you are just moments away from your breakthrough and are ready to come back out in this second half and dominate. Others of you need to make the decision right now to pull that uniform back out of the closet, the one with your name on it...TAKE PRIDE IN WHO YOU ARE. Lace 'em up and get back on the field of life, baby.

This is the most important game you will ever play in and you have fans, teammates and a crowd of people cheering you on who need you to WIN so that they can win, baby.

> **"The harder the conflict, the more glorious the triumph."**
>
> Thomas Paine

Today you will GET BACK IN THE GAME. Today you will come out for the second half STRONG. Today you will make the decision to FIGHT until you are FIT FOR LIFE.

Here are your three R's to GET BACK IN THE GAME:

1. RECOGNIZE – What needs to be improved? What areas do you need to make adjustments in? Just like a successful team, at halftime you must evaluate the first half and be truthful about what needs to be changed. The first key to change is to RECOGNIZE what is wrong and what needs to be improved upon.

2. REFOCUS – Take some time to REFOCUS. Refocus on the goal and the end game. Refocus on what needs to be done right now to WIN. Remind yourself of your WHAT, WHY you do what you do, and WHO you are.

3. RAIN – Growing up, I loved rap music. Rappers have this saying, "MAKE IT RAIN." Make it rain to me means, "I am wiling to do whatever needs to be done to WIN." What

97

are you willing to do to WIN, to be YOUR BEST, to be FIT FOR LIFE? Now is the time to MAKE IT RAIN, baby!

Today to be FIT FOR LIFE, you will choose to GET BACK IN THE GAME, RECOGNIZE, REFOCUS AND MAKE IT RAIN.

TAKE ACTION:

In what areas of my life have I been out of the game (physically, mentally, emotionally, spiritually, relationally, financially, professionally)?

What meaning will I choose to give to the things that happen to me in life?

How will I REFOCUS next time when I feel like I am out of the game?

WINNING CONFESSION:

I AM BACK IN THE GAME. Today I WILL choose to JUST DO IT! I AM not moved by what happens to me in life. I CHOOSE to be in control of my life and my response. Nothing in life has meaning except the meaning I CHOOSE to give it. I choose to RECOGNIZE what needs to change in my life today. I choose to REFOCUS on what matters most to me in life today. I choose to MAKE IT RAIN and JUST DO IT today. I AM A WINNER. I AM A HERO. I AM FIT FOR LIFE!

FIT FOR LIFE STORY:

FFR is more than a physical workout for Kyle Zickefoose….it is a mind- shaping experience!

I'm Kyle Zickefoose, I'm 47 years old and I'm a Battalion Chief with the Sapulpa Fire Department.

I would like to say that my favorite part of FFR is the workout, but I really love the coaches! **They are so motivating and knowledgeable!** I keep coming back to FFR because I know there is no other gym in the country that offers the positive atmosphere and caters to first responders like FFR. **It's more than a physical workout, it's also a mind-shaping experience.**

I have seen so many results. My fitness has never been what it is today and at 47, that's saying something. However, **I'd say the biggest improvements I've experienced have been in my frame of mind.**

FFR has changed my life by changing the way I think about a great many things. I now go into the workouts with an attack mode like I never had before. This attitude has transferred over to other aspects of my life for the better. The most important change in me is the way I think and feel about my job, family and friends.

When I started FFR, I was told that I needed a WHY to have focus. I did not have a WHY. I had been on pain pills for arthritis in my neck for the last 2 1/2 years. Because of FFR, I found my WHY and am now pain pill free. I have a new zest for life, family and work. It's really deeper than what I can get into in this short testimonial.

If a first responder will completely buy into the FFR program - but most of all, buy into believing in himself - he will see a change in his physical appearance and his mental impression and he will have the confidence to succeed in all aspects of his life.

Battalion Chief Kyle Zickefoose

Firefighter

CHAPTER EIGHT

OWN THE MOMENT

"Perfection is not attainable, but if we chase perfection we can catch excellence."

Vince Lombardi

FFROnline.TV/Lesson-8

You've heard it before...

People perish for lack of knowledge. I say it a little differently: "People perish for lack of the <u>RIGHT</u> knowledge!" With so much information out there, it's easy to get overwhelmed and overloaded. I want you to focus now on what you really need to know to get you what you want. What do you need to do today to get the RIGHT information, to gain the RIGHT knowledge to get what you truly desire? You will always be a student, constantly learning and growing, but starting today, you will stay focused on OWNING THE MOMENT. Forget about everything else, my friend; there is meaning in the moment, and today you will discover how to be your best and OWN THE MOMENT!

What is it that you need RIGHT now in order to perfect your skill on the job? Many times we get so caught up in the big picture, looking toward the future, that we miss the meaning in the moment. What can you do RIGHT now to be better on the job? What can you do RIGHT now to be better in your household as a spouse or a parent? What can you do today to get closer to the level of physical fitness you want? OWNING THE MOMENT is the discipline to do what needs to be done RIGHT now and the peace of mind that comes from knowing that those small things you do today will take you to the ultimate life you desire. When it comes to training your mindset to be THE BEST version of you, you have the RIGHT FIT FOR LIFE game plan right here in your hands to make it happen.

> **"Lead me, follow me, or get the hell out of my way."**
>
> George S. Patton Jr., *Patton*

You have got to gain a respect for the present moment. Being a great leader and HERO as a first responder is your job and once you begin to feel that your present job is important, you will become enthusiastic about being GREAT. This all starts with maximizing the moment and taking pride in where you currently are. There is a direct correlation between how you feel about your current position and how you perform. Your job RIGHT now is to be the BEST you, you can be as you OWN THE MOMENT. BE THE BEST first responder, parent, spouse, leader, whatever you are called to be, be the best RIGHT NOW!

So many times we get so busy building the future that we miss what's in front of us RIGHT now. Your family needs you now, your friends need you now, your fellow firefighters and your city needs THE BEST YOU now! Don't be so busy that you miss opportunities that are right in front of you that you may never get again. Take time to build new relationships, flourish in your current relationships, gain the right knowledge, put in the work and do what needs to be done to be great. Start to be the greatest student of you in the moment. What are you learning every day to make you a better you? What are you doing each day to OWN THE MOMENT in every environment you are in? Start to become the hardest worker now in your current level, while keeping your eyes on the prize in knowing that OWNING THE MOMENT today will lead you to your promise land.

Today for you to be FIT FOR LIFE, you will develop the discipline and enthusiasm to be YOUR BEST in the moment so that you can OWN THE MOMENT.

TAKE ACTION:

What knowledge do I need to be FIT FOR LIFE (physically, mentally, emotionally, relationally, professionally, financially)?

What things have I missed out on because I was too busy?

In what areas of my life will I commit to OWN THE MOMENT?

WINNING CONFESSION:

I am committed to being the best version of me today. I will OWN THE MOMENT. I will be a great student and invest in being a better me each day. My family needs me! My friends need me! My firefighter brothers and sisters need me! The world needs THE BEST version of me! I AM A HERO! I WILL stay focused and OWN THE MOMENT today. I AM FIT FOR LIFE.

FIT FOR LIFE STORY:

Michael Elliott is dedicated to continuing his FFR success!

I'm Michael Elliott, I'm 42 years old and I'm a Tulsa Police Officer.

My favorite aspect of FFR is definitely the positive environment. It is truly a family and it makes you want to work harder to be your best. The coaches are amazing and they truly care. **The positivity consumes you, and the results are just an added perk.**

My physical results have been amazing. I lost 43 pounds, 8% body fat, and 25.5 inches. The greatest changes for me have been both mental and spiritual. I find myself wanting to be as positive as I possibly can when dealing with my family and the citizens of Tulsa. Since starting FFR, I have forged some strong relationships with fellow officers, firefighters, and EMSA personnel. **Those** relationships absolutely did not exist prior to FFR!

The positive changes I see in my life are great. I like the way I look, but I feel even better. I am more active now than I have ever been in my life. My family is also more active than ever, and we are so much closer.

As for my work life, work is great! We are a much closer department now. In the 10 years I have been in this department, I have never seen such unity. We initially bonded over FFR workouts, but I feel like we are truly concerned about each other personally now. FFR was the catalyst to bring our entire department together.

Going forward, I plan to continue doing exactly what I have been doing executing the FFR daily Winning Game Plan. The changes that I have made in my physical, mental and spiritual self are permanent. **I am dedicated to continuing my success.**

Michael Elliott

Police Officer

CHAPTER NINE

WIN OR LEARN!

"The real glory is being knocked to your knees and then coming back. That's real glory."

FFROnline.TV/Lesson-9

Vince Lombardi

You WIN or you what? You would probably finish that sentence with the word, "Lose!" You win or you lose. Losing is a mindset. The only way you lose is if you accept a loss as defeat. Starting today to be FIT FOR LIFE, you won't accept failure as a loss! You won't lose any longer, baby. To be THE BEST version of you, you MUST learn how to use failure successfully in your life, how to take what may look like a loss and turn it into a WIN.

I don't care what happened in the past and starting today, you won't care either.

Failure is not an option. From here on out, you will establish the no-quit mentality, the no-quit attitude. No matter what the situation may look like at the moment, you will ask yourself the powerful question, "What did I learn about the situation and about myself?"

> "A man must be big enough to admit his mistakes, smart enough to profit from them, and strong enough to correct them."
>
> John C. Maxwell

The only way you fail is if you don't try. The only way you fail is if you don't finish. The only way you lose is if you don't learn. The only way you will ever experience true growth in your life is through failure. To WIN in life, you have to take risks, you have to push the limits of what may be comfortable at the moment.

Starting today, to be FIT FOR LIFE, you will get focused on the prize and commit to NEVER QUIT. Starting today, you will elevate your vision and expand your thinking. Starting today, you will set bigger goals and you will continually push the boundaries so that you can elevate your standard and capabilities to ultimately find new ways to break through and WIN. In failure, you can truly learn as life offers you the greatest opportunity to readjust, reevaluate, improvise, improve, and come back stronger to WIN.

Winston Churchill once said, "Act as though it were impossible to fail." Winners use losses to drive themselves to become better. Quitters take losses and use them as excuses to quit.

Today to be FIT FOR LIFE, you will no longer accept failure as an option, you will no longer view a loss as a lose. You will be committed to only WINNING and learning from here on out.

9 WIN OR LEARN!

TAKE ACTION:

In what areas of my life have I accepted a loss?

In what areas of my life have I accepted failure as an option?

What area of my life will I take a risk in and do something that is uncomfortable to create growth in my life?

WINNING CONFESSION:

I am a WINNER. I only WIN or learn. Failure is not an option in my life. I am committed to reaching my goals. I can do it and I WILL do it! I am not a quitter and nothing can stop me. I have the discipline, the determination and the drive to WIN! I AM FIT FOR LIFE.

FIT FOR LIFE STORY:

Darin Detherow loses 53 pounds to become a top finisher!

I'm Darin Detherow, I'm 35 years old, I'm a Fire Equipment Operator for the City of Tulsa and I was a top finisher in our 25-week Truck Challenge for Fit First Responders.

My favorite aspect of FFR is the atmosphere. The amount of positive energy the coaches and fellow FFR members bring with every workout is second to none. Even in the wee hours of the morning, they inspire me to push myself to give 100% effort, 100% of the time. The results you get by pushing one another in a group atmosphere cannot be replicated. The coaches' ability to inspire, motivate, and put things into perspective is really what separates this program from any other program like it out there.

Since the beginning of the competition, I have transformed my body physically, losing over 53 pounds and dropping 12 inches off my waist size. I have gained physical strength that I didn't think possible. I increased my max bench press by 25 pounds, deadlift by 90 pounds, and have gained three inches in flexibility. **But even better is the way this program has transformed my overall health. After 23 long years, I am no longer a slave to chewing tobacco nor do I have to rely on medication to regulate my blood pressure.**

Mentally, I now feel there is nothing I cannot accomplish. Once I set my mind on a goal, I know it will be attained. I have also gained a new respect for the other first responding agencies. **The fact that we all went through this challenge together built**

a respect that has carried over to the streets. This program has undoubtedly transformed my way of thinking for the better. It has made me analyze every aspect of my life and has allowed me to see what negative things I can do without.

All of these things are huge steps in the right direction to living a fuller and happier life, but forget all of that. What I am most proud of are the little WINS with my kids and wife at home. Besides being firefighters, most of my colleagues work a second job in order to pay the bills. I mow lawns on my days off. So after working a 24-hour shift at the fire station, I mow lawns outside in the heat for 6 – 7 hours before I go home. In years past, I would be so tired all I would want to do is go home, shower, and lie on the couch to recover. Now, I go outside and jump on the trampoline or push my kids on the swing, sometimes until dark. Let me tell you, when your two-year-old son goes from wanting little to do with you because you were too busy or too exhausted to play with him before, to now grabbing your hand and telling you that you are his best friend...**it makes all of this effort worthwhile!**

This program is infectious. Now that my mindset has changed, I can see the positive effects spreading like wildfire to other people in my life. My wife has lost 24 pounds in the last 10 weeks. My brother and two other friends now meet on the weekends to work out together. It just seems the more I better myself, the more everyone around me wants to do the same.

Improving myself physically, mentally, and financially has now become an OBSESSION! An obsession that I love.

The Fit First Responder family has shown me how to take control of my physical health and improve my habits, but even more importantly, **it has shown me how to change my thinking. I have learned that all change begins with the mindset, how YOU perceive the situation YOU are in! FFR has been a game changer for me!**

Going forward, I intend to use the knowledge and habits formed at FFR to continue bettering myself and the people around me.

Darin Detherow

Fire Equipment Operator

CHAPTER TEN

NO MORE EXCUSES

"It's the moment you truly discover the amazing calling on your life that all excuses become obsolete."

FFROnline.TV/Lesson-10

Coach JC

No great HERO has ever become great by making excuses. You will make the choice today to no longer make excuses in your life. Excuses are easy and many times convenient, until you truly understand your purpose and calling in life.

It's time to take responsibility for YOU! It's your body, your career, your life! This is such a powerful thing because if you fail to take responsibility, you will look at your life as a failure, keep making excuses, and never accomplish your dreams and goals. Once you take responsibility, you will begin to experience peace and joy in your life as you take full control over every situation. It's time to be honest with yourself. Starting today, eliminate words like I can't, but, someday, and tomorrow from your vocabulary!

Did you know that before the time you graduated from first grade, you heard the word "no" over 40,000 times? That's right! That is in comparison to hearing the word "yes" only 5,000 times. You have been conditioned into a "no" environment. Starting today, that has got to change. Start to create your "yes" environment.

> **"Face reality as it is, not as it was or as you wish it to be."**
>
> Jack Welch

Don't accept the thought of no, can't, impossible, maybe, and all those other words that question whether your dreams and goals are going to become a reality. Stay focused on what you can control and rid yourself of those things that are controlling your emotions, distracting your actions and stealing your concentration. The WINNING CONFESSIONS in this game plan are designed to help you create your "yes" environment. Create your "yes" environment today!

The words you use influence your mind and condition your actions. Your words make excuses for why you can't do something or have something. The words you choose to use will determine the direction you go mentally and physically.

I once heard it said, "Don't believe everything you hear, even if you're the one doing all the talking." Starting today, you have got to become aware of the words you use when speaking to others and yourself. Whenever that voice in your head says, "I can't," ask yourself two simple questions: Where are the facts and evidence that prove I can't? Has anyone else ever been able to make this happen?

Stop talking yourself out of getting what you truly desire. What's more important: your excuse or your desire? You can only have one - excuses or RESULTS. You cannot have both. What do you choose? Stop playing the blame game. TAKE RESPONSIBILITY knowing that if you don't have what you desire, it is no one else's fault but yours.

Mentally strong HEROES become self motivated and don't accept excuses. Start today to enter every day and every situation to WIN. Start today to believe that you are the BEST player in the game, at the station and in your household. No longer allow yourself to think self-defeating, excuse making thoughts.

Today to be FIT FOR LIFE, you will WIN THE DAY by no longer making excuses in your life.

TAKE ACTION:

What area of my life will I take responsibility for, starting today?

What excuses have I allowed myself to make in life?

What will I take action on starting today?

WINNING CONFESSION:

I am a mentally strong HERO. I choose to take responsibility for my words, my actions and my life. I am committed to WINNING and I don't accept or make excuses. I choose to speak positive uplifting words about my life and my career. I WILL WIN today. I am FIT FOR LIFE.

FIT FOR LIFE STORY:

Stewart Andrew says Fit First Responders is his best decision in a long time!

I am currently a NREMT-P FTO at EMSA in Tulsa, Oklahoma. I have been at EMSA for five years, but the last two years have been the best two years. This is because I have been a member of FFR since October 2014. Before FFR, I had let myself go in all aspects of life. I wasn't the best husband or father and I had become complacent with who I was. I lacked drive and passion.

I experienced amazing physical results during the 25-week truck challenge. I lost 22.7 pounds, 12.1% body fat, 26.2 Body Fat Mass (or pounds of fat), and 16.5 inches. **I gained lean muscle mass, increased endurance, increased flexibility, and dropped four pant sizes...plus got abs!!!**

The changes that I made as a result of FFR are now habits and my whole family is healthier. My kids ask for water instead of juice. My wife and I communicate better. Yes, we still struggle at times, but overall we work better as a team now. Just implementing into my everyday life the 4 pillars we are taught to be FIT FOR DUTY has made a huge difference. Physically, mentally, emotionally, spiritually...I am just a better version of me.

My strength at work has improved tremendously. For instance, recently we transported a patient home from the hospital with a complaint of weakness. The patient weighed 260 pounds and was unable to step up into his house himself. I was able to get him all the way into his house and into his bed. The exercises we do in FFR translate very well to our jobs, and I realize this every time my strength and endurance is tested. I am far from perfect, but I do a much better job of taking care of the important things that I used to neglect.

My favorite aspect of Fit First Responders is the lifelong friendships I have built with first responders within the different services in my city. If you are first responder, FFR is for you. **As a result of my success, I have personally been able to encourage over 30 EMSA medics to join FFR!** I plan to continue to do what I have already been doing, working out at least four to five times a week. I would encourage anyone reading this who is on the fence about being better in life to join FFR now. It has been the best decision I have made in a long time. I have no regrets. I am fit for duty, fit for life.

Stewart Andrew

Nationally Registered Emergency Medical Technician

Paramedic Field Training Officer

SECTION THREE: THE **ACTIONS** YOU WILL NOW TAKE

CHAPTER ELEVEN

ARE YOU A PLAYER

"Accountability is making the decision to become REAL with yourself, REAL with what you want and to allow others to make you great by becoming REAL with them!"

FFROnline.TV/Lesson-11

Coach JC

ARE YOU A PLAYER? Every winning team is made up of players at many different positions, starting with the head coach and going all the way down to the manager. Each player brings value and has their role in helping the team win. Just because you are on the team doesn't make you a player. So I want to ask you again, ARE YOU A PLAYER? A player brings value to a team. A player knows his role and executes it effectively day in and day out. A player makes his teammates better.

At our non-profit, Fit First Responders, we have been blessed to serve hundreds of the finest and bravest HEROES (just like you) in our nation. We have seen tremendous physical, mental, emotional, spiritual, and relational results as we've taught these HEROES to win on the job and off of the job, but I can honestly say that the greatest result we've seen has been in the area of unity. We've seen our first responders from over 40 different agencies unify, working together and building a successful team. We have had chiefs of police and fire on many occasions mention that they felt this was the greatest they have ever seen their agency work together. A team without unity is a team divided.

> **"The nation will find it very hard to look up to the leaders who are keeping their ears to the ground."**
>
> Sir Winston Churchill

Are you a player? Are you doing what you need to do to bring THE BEST you to the team, or are you the weakest link? What value do you bring to the team? There is a great book that I would love for you to read called, You Win in the Locker Room First, by Jon Gordon. In this book, Jon gives you the 7 C's to build a winning team. I have been honored to spend some time in departments and stations all over our country and one of the reasons that this book was written was to help create stronger players and stronger teams within the agencies. The vision was for first responders to use this game plan as a tool to take time each day to personally develop and build that strong team of HEROES.

Today I am going to give you my 3 C's to be THE BEST PLAYER you can be.

1. COMMIT. Commit to be ALL IN. You cannot go by how you feel and WIN in life. Commit to be ALL IN. You will never like everything about every player on your team, but you must commit to BE YOUR BEST to give each player on your team a chance. So today, I want for you to commit to overcome any preconceived ideas, thoughts and feelings you may have towards the other players on your team. Today you will need to commit to forget what has happened in the past and move on. Today you will need to commit to be ALL IN to make the house a better place than how you found it.

2. COMMUNICATE. How do you expect to build a better team if all you ever do is break others down? Communication is key to building a great team. Most of us have never been taught how to communicate. You can have disagreements and not always view things the same way, especially in the areas of politics, sports teams, morals, and religion, but you must still choose to communicate and not judge. Communication comes down to two things. You must make a decision to FULLY HEAR and FULLY UNDERSTAND. You may not always agree, but you must make sure that you fully hear what your teammate is wanting to tell you and you must try to fully understand their point of view. To WIN on a team, you have to commit to not name call or break down a teammate, but rather build up and edify them.

3. CONNECT. Making contact is a one-time thing; connection is a lifetime thing. How can you just coexist in the same house as a family member? Yet you see this in marriages, with kids and parents and you even see it in fire stations. Today, you will connect by becoming accountable. So many people get uncomfortable when they hear the word "accountability," but you will only go as far as you make yourself accountable! Who are you allowing to hold you accountable? Being accountable is a great thing and it is a must for you to reach your goals and get what you desire! Look at almost every successful athlete in life and you will find that they had true accountability throughout the process of achieving their success.

NO ONE at FFRONLINE.tv does life alone! Tough times will occur, obstacles will arise, and adversity will come at you; this is when that accountability relationships in your life will be able to pull you through. You have to be accountable! There will be times when you slip up in life. It's at these times when accountability is a MUST, to remind you why you do what you do and to keep you focused on your goal.

This does not mean that I am telling you to trust everyone and anyone. What I am telling you is to find someone you trust and respect and allow them to make you better. This is someone who wants to see you achieve your goals and live your life to the fullest. No one cares about you getting what you truly desire as much as you, but this person or people may come in a close second at wanting to see you succeed. This is someone you can be totally open, honest, and vulnerable with at all times.

Accountability is simple if you really want to WIN in life and be FIT FOR LIFE. If you think you have arrived or want to let your pride stand in the way, then accountability may not be that simple for you.

Here's how it works: Tell your accountability partner your goals in being FIT FOR LIFE and the game plan that you will use to get that thing you desire. You will then keep each other motivated and focused on the prize and not let each other quit. You will talk about the WINS in life and also be real about the struggles of life. Just as iron sharpens iron, accountability partners sharpen each other.

Today to be FIT FOR LIFE, you will be a player and choose to be accountable and hold others accountable.

TAKE ACTION:

I will commit today to no name calling, slander, gossip or hate within our team.

Each day, I will choose to COMMUNICATE with myteam and make it a point to see that they are fully heard and fully understood.

Who will I CONNECT with today to be accountable to?

WINNING CONFESSION:

TODAY, I will be a PLAYER. I choose to COMMIT to be all in to make my team better. I will COMMUNICATE with my teammates in an uplifting and positive way. I will CONNECT and choose to be accountable. I AM FIT FOR LIFE!

FIT FOR LIFE STORY:

Terry Sivadon knew in his heart that FFR was the program for him!

My life before Fit First Responders was just mediocre. In one way, it was great because I had just gotten married to the love of my life. On the other hand, I was not happy with myself. I knew I was overweight, would get out of breath easily and I was worried about being able to do my job as a firefighter. I had high blood pressure, high cholesterol, and back and shoulder pain that would keep me awake at night. I tried to be active and work out, but with no extra time at the fire station and making no time at home, it was not happening. I had a membership to a local gym, but I never went. I knew something had to be done, but I did not know where to start.

After 25 weeks of FFR, I feel 100% better!!! I feel stronger. I am much more active. I have much more energy, and **I am pain free. I am no longer taking medication for high blood pressure or high cholesterol.** Mentally, I am much more positive about life. I am very confident in my ability to perform everyday tasks, whether they are at work or home. **Spiritually,** I have taken up the role of spiritual leader of my family. I have spent more time in prayer and have become more grateful for God's gifts. **Relationally,** I have become more social with my family, friends and co-workers and more active with my kids. My relationship with my wife is amazing, because when I feel better, she feels better.

The FFR program has been life changing for me. FFR has been a Godsend because I knew I desperately needed to make changes. A few days before Coach JC came to my fire station, I was sitting at the table talking to my guys about how I needed to do something. I was very upset with myself because I didn't know where to start. I knew diets did not work, but I did not know what to do. A couple of shifts later, Coach JC walked into my fire station to tell us about the Fit First Responders program. Our station was the first station they visited! It was definitely a God thing! **I knew in my heart that this was the program for me.**

As a firefighter, FFR has made a huge difference in my work life. No one can beat me to the fire truck when a drop hits. I am setting the standard for my crew! When your intensity and ability is high, it tends to increase everyone else's performance. When I get up in the middle of the night now, I have no pain in my back or shoulders and I am able to perform my job so much better. I have 22 years on the job and was looking at retiring at 25 years in. Now, I can work for 30-plus years, easily!!

FFR has been a life-changing event for me. There is no way I will go back to the way I was. I am going to keep winning with my health and nutrition. I am focusing on my strength and on helping others WIN in life. My role as a motivator and a mentor has brought several new participants to the program. I want to be a part of the growth of the FFR program across the nation. **I am honored to be a part of the Fire Advisory Committee.**

Captain Terry Sivadon
Firefighter

CHAPTER TWELVE

HIT IT!

"Be not deceived; God is not mocked: for whatsoever a man sows, that shall he also reap."

FFROnline.TV/Lesson-12

Galatians 6:7, King James Version

HIT IT! Now is your time! HIT IT! What I sow is what I shall reap! This is not just some spiritual saying from the Bible, but a universal law in life. I have found it to be very true in many different aspects of life. What you sow, you will reap. If you sow bad stuff, you will reap bad stuff; if you sow good stuff, you will reap the reward. If all you eat is junk food, you will reap the negative effects of that junk food. If you sow the time to train and work on your skill as a first responder, you will become great and move up in ranking. HIT IT!

Everyone wants success. Most people want to WIN. As a HERO, I know that you desire to BE YOUR BEST so you are FIT FOR LIFE or you wouldn't be reading this right now. Everyone wants to be successful, but those who achieve success are sowing the right seed every single day. Those successful athletes, those successful marriages, those successful businesses, those winning in their fitness and health, they all have one thing in common... they sowed the seed to get that success! They are disciplined and determined to do what needs to be done, day in and day out, to WIN. They HIT IT! They do what they have to do, when they have to, even when they don't feel like doing it.

> "Men make history and not the other way around. In periods where there is no leadership, society stands still. Progress occurs when courageous, skillful leaders seize the opportunity to change things for the better."
>
> Harry S. Truman

Having a big dream is not enough. Wanting to make more money is not enough. The desire to get that promotion, have that thriving marriage, transform your body and increase your fitness and health is not enough. That desire is a MUST, but it is not enough. You must be driven and willing to invest each day into your most valuable player. YOU ARE THE MVP! The self-disciplined first responder who accepts no excuses, has complete resolve to be FIT FOR LIFE, and executes the daily rituals, is the one who WINS. This is how you SEPARATE YOURSELF! This is how you become FIT FOR LIFE!

How much time are you sowing into getting what you want? Are your daily actions lining up with what you say

you want? Ask yourself right now, "ARE MY DAILY AC-
TIONS LINING UP WITH WHAT I SAY I WANT?" What
are your daily habits? How much effort are you sowing into
your daily action steps to get what you desire? What do your
daily rituals look like?

HIT IT! There is no better time than now! You don't
have to wait to feel 100% like doing it. Just do it! HIT IT!
It doesn't have to be perfect; just get moving, baby! Are
you sowing the right seed? Stop wasting your time staying
busy and start investing your time to get closer to being FIT
FOR LIFE! Start today to make sure that you are sowing the
RIGHT seed on a daily basis to reap the ultimate reward as
the HERO that you are. You are a HERO! You deserve to BE
YOUR BEST and be FIT FOR LIFE.

To be FIT FOR LIFE, you have got to eliminate daily distractions. I have met so many first responders who lead con-
flicting lives. They say they want one thing, but they are just
not willing to do what it takes to get it. Don't be deceived
into thinking these distractions will not keep you from WIN-
NING. Eliminate distractions in your life that you know are
keeping you from being YOUR BEST.

"If you want something you have never had, you must be willing to do something you have never done."

Thomas Jefferson

Today to be FIT FOR LIFE, you will HIT IT. You will start today to be disciplined and invest the time every day to sow the actions necessary to WIN.

TAKE ACTION:

What do I desire to reap?

What one disciplined thing will I sow every day to make this happen?

What am I going to do that I've never done so that I can get what I've never had?

WINNING CONFESSION:

I am a HERO. I deserve to WIN. I choose today to make sure my daily actions line up with what I say I want. I will HIT IT, even when I don't feel 100% like it. I AM DISCIPLINED! I AM DETERMINED! I was born to WIN and today, I will start to sow good seed so I can reap the reward. I AM FIT FOR LIFE!

FIT FOR LIFE STORY:

Joe Gamboa says FFR was a complete game changer!

I would like to talk you about a program that is a complete game changer. A program that will bring out the best in you. A program that will motivate you and give you the edge you need to be more confident on the job.

I am a police officer and I wear many hats in my job. I am a SWAT operator with the Special Operations Team, an investigator, a trainer, a mentor, a teacher and a leader. To be the best at my job requires me to be multifaceted and well-rounded in many different disciplines. I have to know case law, I have to be a high level marksman and I also have to be in top physical condition.

I have always known that as a police officer, I am responsible for my own physical fitness. I have always done something like running, martial arts or weightlifting to stay in shape. Nobody else should have to carry me or my equipment. **I always thought I was in good shape until I started at FFR.**

133

They train you like an athlete and challenge you to be better than when you walked in the door. They will take you to the limit and beyond. I no longer train for events such as The Goruck Tough, The Tough Mudder or the Gauntlet. I don't have to because I am ready for them at any time because of what FFR has done to me. This also tells me that I am ready for any challenges I may face at work.

Because of how I have physically changed, I am a better marksman. Actually, I am more consistent with my weapons. The physical nature of my job is not a factor for me. If my job requires me to climb a fence with gear and weapons on, then I do it. If my job requires me to pick up a person and get them to safety, then I do it. If my job requires me to run a distance and shoot with accuracy, then I do it. If my job requires me to run in a burning house with an armed suspect to save a life, then I do it.

Last year I went through an air assault course for law enforcement. The course required me to put in long hours doing land navigation, a road march, daily PT, and rappelling from a helicopter. I never trained one day for the course and yet I had the stamina to earn my air assault wings.

A few weeks ago, I started squatting 315 pounds and front squatting 225, both of which I never thought I would do. I am five feet eight and one half inches tall and weigh between 175 to 183. I am 44 years old and I try my best to compete hard, fast and strong every day I am alive.

I changed my mindset. I do this training because I want to save a life, I want to be there for another first responder and most importantly, I want to come home to my family.

Bottom line, don't be impressed by what I have accomplished or what I can do. Be impressed by what this program can do for you. Be impressed when you find yourself alone only to realize it's because you're in first place.

Success happens because you know what it means to fail.

Joe Gamboa II

Special Operations Team

Police Officer

CHAPTER THIRTEEN

BE YOUR BEST

"Are you willing to sacrifice what you want MOST IN LIFE for what you want at the moment?"

FFROnline.TV/Lesson-13

Coach JC

BE YOUR BEST! How badly do you really want it? How badly do you really want to be FIT FOR LIFE? How badly do you really want to WIN physically, mentally, emotionally, spiritually, relationally, financially, and on the job as a first responder? How badly do you really want to BE YOUR BEST? Now is your time! All it takes is one choice. Just one decision – made by you – RIGHT NOW!

"I WILL NOT TRADE WHAT I WANT MOST IN LIFE FOR WHAT I WANT AT THE MOMENT!"

That is it! One of the most important questions that you will ask yourself on a daily basis so that you can BE YOUR BEST is, "AM I WILLING TO TRADE WHAT I WANT MOST IN LIFE FOR WHAT I WANT AT THE MOMENT?" This powerful question will help keep you FOCUSED so that you can

BE YOUR BEST. Think about it... every single day, there are things put in front of us to take us off track, to distract us from our purpose in life. Every single day, there are tempting, cool, sexy, shiny objects right in front of us that we can have at the moment. For instance, you just started eating clean and that local donut shop, out of the goodness of their heart, delivers three dozen donuts to the station. WHAT?! You are trying to stay focused on your marriage and that other person keeps popping up in your mind, tempting you to cheat on your spouse.

To BE YOUR BEST, you must not allow what is convenient, sexy, tempting, and cool at the moment to control you. You are not controlled by your emotions, you control what you do and how you respond. This is why we start in the first few chapters by discovering your WHAT. If you don't know what you want, you will trade all day long for what your flesh wants at the moment.

What do you want? No! WHAT DO YOU REALLY WANT? You better know, my friend, and you better stay steadfast in investing into that thing every day. Ask yourself that powerful question and answer it honestly to BE YOUR BEST – "AM I WILLING TO TRADE WHAT I WANT MOST IN LIFE FOR WHAT I WANT AT THE MOMENT?"

I have visited with so many first responders who wanted to do great things and wanted to be their best, but just got caught up with the wrong people, caught up watching the wrong things, caught up with the wrong thoughts, caught up with that side chick, caught up with that addiction. They were caught up with what was appealing at the moment. The temptation will never stop, my friend, but I do have great news for you. YOU HAVE WHAT IT TAKES. You are better than that. The calling on your life is for good and not for evil. You were bought with a price and YOU ARE WORTH IT! Don't get caught up. Now is the time to BE YOUR BEST!

> **"The human voice can never reach the distance that is covered by the still, small voice of conscience."**
>
> Mahatma Gandhi

Much of life is a routine, and I have seen a lot of first responders give into temptations because they became stale and stagnant in their daily routines. If you are not careful, it is very easy to fall into this trap of complacency, which then leads to compromise. Make a decision today that you are not going to live another day on cruise control. Make a decision today that you are not going to allow your life to become stagnant. Have some passion about who you are, and make the decision to be passionate about what you are doing. It's your choice! Yes, it is that simple.

BE YOUR BEST! Don't get caught up and allow compromising decisions to mold your future. You may not feel your best right now, you may put up a front on the outside while you're losing on the inside, you may have been living that double life of confusion and compromise for so long that you feel like you're stuck. NOW IS YOUR TIME! Rise up! BE YOUR BEST! Just one decision, baby! Just say, "I am done trading what I want most in life for what I want at the moment. I am done being average! I am done being mediocre. I AM DONE!"

Today, choose to take control of your life by no longer compromising who you are, what you stand for and what you are about. Today, choose to take control of your life by understanding your value and worth. You choose what your life looks like. You choose how much money you make. You choose what religion you practice. You choose what kind of marriage you have. You choose the legacy you leave as a first responder. You choose just about everything that happens on a daily basis. You choose who you are. You choose what you do. And today, you are choosing to BE YOUR BEST!

Starting today, I want you to make the decision that your life is valuable and that you are worth it. You are done compromising! Starting today, you will no longer make excuses, and you will no longer accept anything but GREATNESS. You will no longer accept anything but you being YOUR BEST!

Today to be FIT FOR LIFE, you will choose to BE YOUR BEST and not compromise who you are and what you stand for.

"Am I willing to trade what I want most
in life for what I want at the moment?"

TAKE ACTION:

What do I want most in life (physically, mentally, emotionally, spiritually, relationally, financially, professionally)?

What choices have I made that compromised who I am
and what I stand for?

In what area of my life do I need to "dig deep" and take
back control so that I can BE MY BEST?

WINNING CONFESSION:

Starting today, I make the decision that my life is valuable and that I am worth it. I will no longer compromise, and I will no longer accept anything else but GREATNESS. I will cut ties with all excuses, idols, relationships, and anything in my life that is holding me back from being my best. Starting today, I choose to make the RIGHT choices that are going to get me what I want. I choose today to no longer trade what I want most in life for what I want at the moment. I WILL BE MY BEST! I AM FIT FOR LIFE!

FIT FOR LIFE STORY:

Alan Hancock says through Fit First Responders, he is joined up with a great group of people who push him to be THE BEST him.

I'd always been intrigued about Fit First Responders (FFR) after the amazing results I'd heard about from many of my co-workers, but I doubted that the program would be beneficial to me in any way. I played soccer and ran track in high school, then continued my track career through college. Because of this, I thought that I knew what it took to be successful, to be fit, and to be able to handle what life threw at me.

I'd begun to notice a downward trend in my fitness and activity level. Along with that, my energy level began to decrease and my attitude turned more negative. I had less fuel in the tank to chase my kids in the yard. I hadn't been giving my wife the time and attention she needed and deserved. I realized I was not giving all that I had in the important areas of my life and that needed to change quickly.

I joined FFR and can say that I've greatly benefitted from all it has to offer. I thought I was just joining a fitness program or another gym. I did gain a gym, but I also gained a lot more. I am now involved with a great group of people who daily push me to be the best version of me that I can be. The coaches around me are invested in me, but not just in my physical results. Though those are important, nutrition, family life, focus, and my faith are also challenged. It'd be easy for a fitness coach to come in and motivate all of us to lift heavy weight, build bigger biceps and return again to repeat the next day. What I've found in my friends at FFR, though, is that I've got a foundation, not only through my increased fitness, but in the aspects of my life that I didn't know were also needing improvement.

"Fit for Duty - Fit for Life" is often heard from the coaches throughout a workout, and this phrase could not be more true to the mentality of everyone involved. I've been challenged to work and train harder, thus making me better equipped for my job as a firefighter. More importantly, I've been challenged to be a better dad, a better husband, and a better person all around. I truly feel that FFR is more than a gym, and it has given me the encouragement and motivation to be the best version of me that I could possibly be. I am confident that I am Fit for Duty. I am even more confident that I am **Fit for Life!**

Alan Hancock

Fire Equipment Operator / Paramedic

CHAPTER FOURTEEN

I'M DONE

"Don't let the noise of others' opinions drown out your own inner voice."

Steve Jobs

FFROnline.TV/Lesson-14

What negative influences are holding you back from being FIT FOR LIFE and accomplishing your goals? Today, you will make the decision to be DONE.

"I'M DONE." Starting today, it's time to eliminate negativity from your life! You know what I'm talking about! Negativity comes from all different places. We are bombarded with it on a daily basis. Other people, the media, what you read, what you listen to and even your own thoughts can and will, if you allow them to, rule your life and keep you from winning.

You need to identify those negative things and start today to eliminate them from your life. Maybe you need to break some negative patterns or habits that you have created. These habits could include things you do, read, or watch – things that may be robbing you of your valuable time. Maybe it's someone in your life who has told you, "You can't do it," or maybe it's the environment that you are in on a daily basis that is holding you back.

These negative forces in your life, both internal and external, will continue to drain you and hold you back from what you truly deserve. It all comes down to one word, my friend, CHOICE! Choose today to change the things you are doing, dissociate from negative people, change your environment, and do whatever you need to do to commit to BE DONE with negativity in your life!

> **"Don't let what you cannot do interfere with what you can do."**
>
> John Wooden

Great HEROES are able to do what they have to do to control their emotions and actions. You can't allow outside sources to affect you. Stop giving attention to the things you can't control and to those negative things that are trying to bring you down.

Today to be FIT FOR LIFE, you will WIN THE DAY by choosing to be DONE with negativity in your life.

TAKE ACTION:

What negative things in my life have been holding me back and what will I replace them with, starting today?

Negative habits?

Replace with:

Negative individuals?

Replace with:

Negative environment?

Replace with:

WINNING CONFESSION:

YES! I CAN! I WILL! It's possible! I am in control of my emotions and my actions. I choose to surround myself with POSITIVE, UPLIFTING people. I choose to no longer allow negative influences in my life. I will only think positive thoughts, speak positive words, and take positive action. I WILL WIN today. I AM FIT FOR LIFE!

FIT FOR LIFE STORY:

Detective Lori Visser loses 26 inches in 25 weeks!

I'm Detective Lori Visser, I'm 55 years old and I've been with the Tulsa Police Department for 25 years.

My results with FFR are phenomenal. I have lost 33 pounds and 8.2% body fat (32 of the 33 pounds was fat loss). I gained some muscle but also lost almost three inches in the neck, six and a half inches in the chest, almost six inches in the waist, six inches in the hips, three and a half inches in the thighs and two inches in the upper arms. **This is a total of 26 ½ inches lost!!**

FFR has made such a huge difference in my life. Losing 33 pounds has motivated me to continue and maintain this lifestyle. After learning that I lost 33 pounds, getting below the 200-pound mark for the first time in 15 years, I became so emotional. Seven months ago, I never dreamed I would be where I am today, moving forward and feeling better than I have in years. I am completely ecstatic about the changes that FFR has helped me realize.

But weight loss and inches lost are not the only physical results I've experienced. My blood pressure is the lowest it has been in many years. My knees have improved and no longer swell when I work out. My energy level has increased tremendously, and my marriage is the best it has been in years. In fact, my husband also lost 30 pounds with me and is eating healthier. I feel stronger, not just physically, but also emotionally and spiritually.

I am grateful to have such experienced and knowledgeable coaches at Fit First Responders. They not only train you to properly lift weights and exercise, but their knowledge of nutrition, supplements and how to take care of your body is phenomenal. **I LOVE that teamwork is a part of the workout.** Saying a prayer at the end of the workout is one of the greatest things and really brings the groups closer together. I look forward to the fellowship each day. **FFR has become family to me and a support that I need to help me achieve my goals in life.**

Thanks to FFR, I am a much better person, a better Christian, a better wife, a better mother, a better grandmother, a better daughter and sister, and a better police officer.

FFR has made a huge difference in my work life. I work

with a much clearer mind. My use of sick leave has gone down. The City of Tulsa wins every day that a police officer, firefighter, or EMSA medic works out at FFR.

During the program, I put in for the IMT (Incident Management Team), and after a successful oral interview, I made the team. I have become much more confident than I was before. It feels great to see people I haven't seen in a while and hear them say, "Lori, what are you doing? You look great!" **I found that I am continuously telling my co-workers about FFR and trying to get them into the program. It works for me and I want it to work for others. I cannot say enough positive about FFR.**

FFR is the BEST thing that has happened to me in years.

I plan to continue doing what I have been doing with FFR, continuing my workouts and maintaining my healthier eating habits. I know that I have a way to go in weight loss, but there is light at the end of the tunnel. This has become my lifestyle and I know that what I dream can be done because I have seen the results. I want to pay it forward by helping others who are overweight like me.

Detective Lori Visser

Police Officer

CHAPTER FIFTEEN

LET IT GO!

"Only the strong know the difference between giving up and letting go."

FFROnline.TV/Lesson-15

You have a past; I have a past; we all have a past. Your past can be your worst enemy or your biggest ally. You can allow your past to haunt you and hold you back from great success on the job and in life, or you can use it to shape you to do great things, get what you deserve and be FIT FOR LIFE.

I have seen so many first responders who just could not let go of the past, and they allowed their past to control their future. I don't care what happened yesterday or 10 years ago, it's done! LET IT GO! We all have situations in our lives that have caused us to become discouraged and develop an attitude of, "It's not worth it," or "What's the point in trying any longer?" **Why allow something that is now out of your control to control you?** You may have failed in a relationship, you may have not been the best on the job, you may have made some bad mistakes, someone may have done you wrong, or something may have happened to you as a kid... LET IT GO! Don't allow feelings of depression, guilt, shame, or anxiety to control you any longer. If you live in the past, you will not be able to fully live in the present or in the future. YOU ARE A HERO! The world needs what you have. Why be controlled by something you cannot control?

> "I have learned that success is to be measured not so much by the position that one has reached in life as by the obstacles which one has overcome while trying to succeed."
>
> Booker T. Washington

Starting today, you will use your past to create future WINS. I want you to think of a past situation that may be holding you back right now, and I want you to ask yourself, "What did I learn from that situation?" You can take any situation, good or bad, and make it a learning experience. Past memories, good or bad, are a part of us. The key is to realize that they are not the reality of who you are right now and then use these past memories to your advantage. So, what did you learn? Maybe you learned that you could have done something differently to get a different result, maybe put yourself into a different environment, or you could have reacted differently to the situation. What could you have done differently? What did you do wrong? What did you do right? I once heard it said, "A smart man learns from his own mistakes; a wise man learns from the mistakes of others." Learn from mistakes and allow what you've learned to propel you to the next chapter of life so that you can be FIT FOR LIFE.

Past memories, good or bad, are a part of who you are but do not define WHO YOU ARE, who you will be or who you can become! Free yourself. Take the garbage out, baby! Throw the chains off; YOU ARE FREE! LET IT GO!

Today to be FIT FOR LIFE, you will choose to no longer focus on the past. You will be committed to being your best today and in the future.

TAKE ACTION:

What past situation or situations have been holding me back?

What have I learned from the past?

What areas will I choose to LET GO today?

WINNING CONFESSION:

I choose today to allow the past to be the past. I AM in complete control and WILL use past failures to create future successes in my life. I WILL be the BEST me in the moment and be a difference maker in the lives of others. I WILL choose the Winning Mindset! I AM FIT FOR LIFE!

FIT FOR LIFE STORY:

Liz Egan says the changes FFR brought to her life were lifesaving for her!

I'm Liz Egan and I'm a 57-year-old veteran of the Tulsa Police Department, currently assigned to the Sex Crimes Unit.

The enthusiasm of the coaching staff at FFR is very important because they had faith in me even when I did not. I always felt like I mattered to the coaches and staff at FFR. I have no doubt their attentiveness in providing the correct exercise form and movements prevented me from having injuries. That this program focuses on high intensity interval training really worked for me in dropping my weight and building muscle. This was unlike any program I had ever tried and the amazing results were unlike any results I had ever achieved. I never tire or grow bored of FFR because the programs are different every day. I always feel like I am learning something new about exercising and what my body can do and achieve. The nutritional expertise was a totally new concept for me and it absolutely worked and was very doable.

FFR gave me all the tools and information to be successful and all I needed to provide was the commitment.

The fellowship and camaraderie that developed between myself and other first responders was paramount because they encouraged me when I did not think I could take another step and or lift another weight. Being amongst peers enabled me to push myself beyond what I thought I was capable of and I encouraged others to do the same.

The physical results for me include a weight loss of 40 pounds, 11 inches off my waist, 12 inches from my hips, and 37.3 of Body Fat Mass lost. I no longer suffer from hypertension or acid reflux and have been off medications for months after starting FFR. The body is a remarkable thing.

Mentally, much like physically, I have more energy. There is an improved clarity and mental focus. I am certainly more positive about myself and this is projected in my interpersonal relationships with others. Since starting FFR, I have had more than one person tell me that I seem happier and more confident. It's true, I actually walk with my head up and shoulders back, with an air of confidence. I am able to contribute more to my community through my volunteer work with shelter dogs because I have the increased energy and motivation to do so.

The changes that FFR made in me were absolutely a life saver, and I am not using that term lightly. I was on a downward spiral in my life. I was dying a slow death from years of weight gain and the maladies that accompany being obese. What FFR has done for me is give my life back on so many levels. God placed FFR in my path at a time when I did not think I mattered to anyone. I mattered to God, and this program and the results it made in my life is evidence of God's love. I will continue to rely on His strength for all things that I do.

FFR has changed my work life. **The confidence gained from being stronger and healthier has impacted the way I interrogate suspects and interview victims of sexual assaults. Having mental clarity and focus during sex crimes investigations is crucial, from the beginning stages of collecting evidence at a crime scene through testifying in court.**

I also know that I can be an effective backer to my fellow officers and perform my duties as the citizens of Tulsa expect. I am acutely aware that if I am on scene with a fellow first responder, I know they have my back and I have theirs.

My plan going forward is to continue with my weight loss and gain more strength and endurance. I want to encourage other first responders to participate in FFR and its challenges. I am hoping that my story and results will be an inspiration and encourage others to take the challenge with FFR. I want to be one of the "OG" mentors in FFR who provide the positive reinforcement to new members to keep them on their path toward a healthy and fit life, just like the OG's before me. So my words to those contemplating the commitment to take the challenge through Fit First Responders is, **"If not...WIN!!!"**

Detective Liz Eagen

Police Officer

SECTION FOUR: TIME TO CREATE YOUR **ATTITUDE**

CHAPTER SIXTEEN

CHECK YOURSELF BEFORE YOU WRECK YOURSELF

"Some people say I have attitude - maybe I do... but I think you have to. You have to believe in yourself when no one else does – that makes you a winner right there."

FFROnline.TV/Lesson-16

Venus Williams

You've heard it said, "Success starts with attitude." I believe that statement is almost right. Your attitude is the second part in your FIT FOR LIFE game plan and it is crucial to your success, but it all starts in your thinking because your mindset leads to your attitude. Your THINKING is what ultimate creates your ATTITUDE; your attitude creates your ACTIONS; your actions will determine your RESULTS; and your results will ultimately dictate what you get out of LIFE.

So why is your attitude so important? Your attitude directly determines your actions! Your attitude affects the way you feel, which impacts how you act. Your attitude will influence how you execute the daily action steps to get to your FIT FOR LIFE lifestyle. Your attitude will directly affect your performance. Your attitude reflects who you are, as what is on the inside comes out. What kind of RESULTS do you want to get? What kind of LIFE do you want to live? Starting today, you will choose to bring the attitude that lines up with getting you what it is you desire.

Mentally tough HEROES like you learn how to remain focused through good times and bad times. Even when things are not going your way, you have got to manage your emotions and set yourself up to WIN. To be FIT FOR LIFE, your attitude has got to be one of, "I'll do what I have to do to WIN! I will not be moved by what I see! I will not allow my emotions to control me!" A winner's attitude is positive, expecting the best even when it doesn't feel like that's what you'll get. There is an, "I can do it" attitude of expectancy that you WILL achieve your dreams, goals and ambitions.

"The price of greatness is responsibility."

Winston Churchill

I once had a first responder just like you walk into my office and say, "Coach, this whole attitude thing that you talked about…I have been working on it and I don't feel like it's working." I remember it like it was yesterday; I paused, looked at him and told him the same thing I'm going to tell you, "YOU DON'T WIN IN LIFE BY GOING BY HOW YOU FEEL!" I can assure you that if you choose to allow your emotions and how you feel at the moment to control you, your attitude will stink.

Your attitude is a choice! Your life will go in the direction that you choose for it to go in. You will have what you choose to have. Life is going to happen. Life is not fair and life is not unfair; life is life! You won't always feel like having a FIT FOR LIFE attitude, but I can assure you that most of what you get out of life is determined by how you CHOOSE to react to each and every circumstance. So make a choice each day to **CHECK YOURSELF BEFORE YOU WRECK YOUR-SELF.** Evaluate whether your attitude is lining up with who you are and what you stand for.

You've heard it said before, "If you think you can, you will, and if you think you can't, you won't." It's YOUR choice! Today to be FIT FOR LIFE, you will choose to check you attitude throughout the day to make sure it lines up with who you are and what you are after.

TAKE ACTION:

My attitude starting today is

I will choose to check my attitude and take ten seconds before I react in the following environments:

WINNING CONFESSION:

I choose today to allow the past to be the past. I AM in complete control and WILL use past failures to create future successes in my life. I WILL be the BEST me in the moment and be a difference maker in the lives of others. I WILL choose the Winning Mindset! I AM FIT FOR LIFE!

FIT FOR LIFE STORY:

Heather and David Weakley just can't get enough of the positive that comes from FFR!

I'm Heather Weakley and I'm 32 years old. And I'm David Weakley and I'm 34 years old. We met each other when we started at the Tulsa Police Academy in 2005. We were married in 2007 and we now have two sons. We are both corporals with the Tulsa Police Department. (Heather is a member of the Incident Management Team, and David is a member of the Special Operations Team.) We became a part of the Fit First Responders program when it first began. We are FFR "OG's."

Our favorite aspect of FFR is that we get to do it together. We are each other's support system and we encourage each other during the time spent training, all while we continue building the teamwork aspect of our relationship. We use each other as a source of encouragement and motivation not only in the gym, but in our life.

Our participation in FFR is not just for us as a married couple, but we also do it for our sons. We want to be good role models for them and teach them the importance and values of living a healthy and active lifestyle and the positive impact it can have on their lives.

We love seeing the results in others as well as ourselves. Seeing someone who is new come into the program, get out of their comfort zone, push it to the limit and achieve life-changing results is extremely motivating. We just can't get enough of the positive that comes from FFR.

Our bodies, minds and relationship have never been healthier! The friendships, support, encouragement and positive atmosphere keep us addicted. Everything in our lives is just better since FFR.

Our jobs are very physically demanding and if we don't take care of our minds and bodies, we would be doing a disservice to the people who count on us. We have both always been actively involved in fitness and have been a part of many different training programs and facilities. While all were great programs, we felt that the FFR program, community and staff best suited our needs and helped produce better results. We've both lost weight and David says he is seeing comparative results and strength numbers that he did when playing college football. Heather is now stronger, faster, and more agile than she's ever been, even after going through a pregnancy and major shoulder surgery. Plain and simple...we are just better versions of ourselves at home and on the job because of the program.

FFR has given us a lot more energy. We are up and playing with our sons more, and it has decreased our work stress. When we are having a rough day because of work, we go to FFR. The workouts and community help us deal with our stresses in a healthy way.

Leading a healthy lifestyle both mentally and physically is contagious! Become that leader and spread it around and let others see it. Don't let physical limitations or negative incidents dictate how you live your life. If you want to make that change or transformation, you have to put forth the effort. Here at FFR, you will have every opportunity and resource available to make the change.

Corporal Dave and Corporal Heather Weakley

Police Officers

CHAPTER SEVENTEEN

ALL IN

"You are either all in or all out...there is no lukewarm in life if you want to WIN!"

Coach JC

FFROnline.TV/Lesson-17

Are you ALL IN? You are a HERO. What you start, you finish. What you say you are going to do, you do. So what are you committed to? These days, it is so easy to not be committed.

Commitment is a choice, not a feeling. Commitment takes sacrifice. Commitment takes effort. What are you truly committed to in life? Everyone wants to WIN, but few are willing to commit.

I would hate to live and die average. Some people have never gone ALL IN... ALL IN in their career, ALL IN in their marriage, ALL IN in their health, ALL IN! Some of us are still stuck in the locker room or on the sideline. Some of us have never played an entire game. **You can't expect to get something you are not willing to give.**

Some of you have never seen what you can fully be because you haven't FULLY thrown yourself at your dream. You signed up for FFRONLINE.tv, but you still haven't fully committed. You are a first responder by title, but you haven't jumped all in yet. You walked down the aisle and said "I do," but you still haven't fully committed in that marriage. WHAT ARE YOU WILLING TO GIVE FOR WHAT YOU WANT TO GET?

"The value of a man should be seen
in what he gives and not in what he
is able to receive."

Albert Einstein

You are either ALL IN or you're out. Casual or COMMIT-TED? Complacent or COMMITTED? If you would really commit yourself, who could you be as a first responder, spouse, parent, entrepreneur? YOU WERE CREATED TO BE A COMMITTED PERSON! To be half committed as a first responder can cost you your life. We don't need any half committed first responders. Are you willing to pay the cost to be committed? GREATNESS is reserved for those who commit.

I have never met anyone who has ever been successful in any area of their life who has not gone through hell, trials, tribulations, tests, sweat and tears, made sacrifices and fought through pain to stay focused and committed. If you have a dream and you commit to it, it will come to pass. You don't win by chance. What are you committed to? What do people get when they get you? Your return is determined by your commitment.

Today to be FIT FOR LIFE, you will choose to be a committed person and do what you say you will do.

TAKE ACTION:

In what areas of my life have I not been "ALL IN"?

My Top Three Commitments are:
(God, Family, Faith, Career, my Dream, etc.)

WINNING CONFESSION:

I choose today to be ALL IN TO WIN! I choose to BE COM-MITTED in life. What I say I will do, I do. What I start, I fin-ish. I AM COMMITTED, SOLD OUT AND ALL IN TO BE MY BEST. I WILL WIN TODAY! I AM FIT FOR LIFE!

FIT FOR LIFE STORY:

Stephen says FFR has been truly LIFE CHANGING.

I weighed 287 pounds. It's embarrassing to admit, but I did. I graduated the academy at 230 pounds and in excellent physical condition. The job and life got to me, though. Injuries, marital problems and other things took a toll.

When I heard some of the firemen and other officers talking about Fit First Responders, my immediate reaction was to push it aside. I witnessed their transformations but lacked the confidence that it would work for me. And besides, it was too far to drive from Sapulpa!

One specific day at work, I remember getting into my patrol car and feeling so uncomfortable because of my body armor. I was convinced that the vest was the cause, but quickly realized it was my bloated gut not being able to expand any further because of the vest. The vest wasn't the problem.

My Brother in Blue talked me into going to FFR and I remember being so nervous on my first day. I didn't want to be embarrassed by all these other people who were in great shape. Once I got through the "VIP" announcement, we started and over the next month, I fought off the urge to vomit during each workout.

It got better. I started losing weight (I've lost 30 pounds so far). I felt better and most importantly, my wife and kids saw the change and encouraged me to keep it up. They have supported me through this and I know they will continue to do so. I can actually go out in the yard and play with my kids without getting winded! That alone has made the workouts worth it.

The support you get from FFR members and coaches is like no other. It truly is life changing. It is what you put into it. You will succeed! Take the step to join and I promise, you won't regret it. There are members who motivate me to keep going and hopefully I am someone's motivation to show up. I fully believe in the motto, FIT FOR DUTY. FIT FOR LIFE. You owe it to yourself, your family, and the community you serve. See ya there!

Sergeant Stephen Zamudio

Police Officer

CHAPTER EIGHTEEN

I AM FEARLESS

"Don't let what you cannot do interfere
with what you can do."

John Wooden

FFROnline.TV/Lesson-18

Fear is a real thing. There are so many things in life that we can fear if we allow ourselves to. The fear of failure, the fear of the unknown, the fear of rejection, the fear of loneliness, the fear of lack, the fear of change, the fear of being judged, the fear of being hurt, or even the fear of success all haunt us. In your profession, the fear of death is a daily real thing. Think about it...how many times in life have you passed up an opportunity because you allowed fear to dictate your decision? Maybe you were scared of rejection, the pressure, the success, or perhaps you were afraid that you just might not be able to do it. Fear can keep you from relationships, opportunities, greater performance, happiness and ultimately from being FIT FOR LIFE. I've been there! Fear can paralyze you right where you're at and can become your worst enemy if you allow it to.

I want to ask you a question: What are you really afraid of? Are you scared that you won't make it? Are you scared that you may not perform once you do make it? Who cares?! Fear can torture you if you don't take control of it now. Fear will prevent you from achieving the FIT FOR LIFE lifestyle you deserve. Think about how many times in your past you knew that you could have done something but did not act out of fear. Really, think about it. What is the worst that could have happened?

Fear will force you to play it safe and will keep you from making big plays in life to WIN. When you're not afraid to fail, your chances of success increase. You can run from fear or you can attack it head on. Start today to view failure as an opportunity to learn and grow. Failure can be a great teacher if you allow it to be.

Did you know that you were only born with two fears? That's right! You were only born with the fear of falling and the fear of loud noises. This is great news for you because that means that all other fears have been created, and if you created them, then YOU can overcome them!

Where does fear come from? You guessed it. It comes from the same place it all starts - in your THINKING! You cannot allow fear to be part of your everyday mindset. Fear is a battle in your mind and today, you will WIN that battle. To overcome fear, you must be real of what that fear is and you must take action to cast it aside immediately.

> "My own definition of leadership is this: The capacity and the will to rally men and women to a common purpose and the character which inspires confidence."
>
> General Montgomery

Today you will make a choice...FAITH OR FEAR? You cannot operate in both fear and faith at the same time. Faith says, "I will not be moved by how I feel. I will not be moved by what I see." Faith is believing and having a hope that it will work out, that you will win. Faith is making the choice to see beyond what the current thought or circumstance may be. Faith is the substance of things hoped for and the evidence of things not seen (Hebrews 11:1).

You may be reading this right now and saying, "Coach JC, my faith has been tested, I've been through the fire, I've been through the flames in life and my faith has been shaken." Well, I've got good news for you, my friend. Faith is not a feeling, it is choice. Today you will choose the Faith Mindset.

Today to be FIT FOR LIFE, you will choose FAITH in your life.

TAKE ACTION:

What has fear kept me from achieving in my life?

What am I afraid of?

What action am I going to take today to overcome this fear in my life?

WINNING CONFESSION:

Today is my day! I will no longer allow fear to control me. I choose FAITH. Whatever I put my hands to WILL succeed. I CAN do anything I set my mind to and I choose to face my fears starting today. I WILL choose the FAITH MINDSET! I AM FEARLESS. I AM FIT FOR LIFE!

FIT FOR LIFE STORY:

Kenny says through FFR, he found the motivation he was looking for in life.

In 2011, I went through a life-altering accident. I spent several days in the hospital undergoing three different procedures to repair a tibia plateau fracture. In the first year after the accident, I had three more surgeries to repair damage. I was in physical therapy for over a year, building my leg muscles and learning how to walk without a limp. Over the course of the surgeries and rehab, **I spiraled into a deep depression and battled with an addiction to pain meds.** I was unable to do much physically, so I continued to gain more weight, which slowed my recovery and got me another prescription because of my high cholesterol.

Being in the military, I am expected to be physically fit and meet certain height and weight requirements. I was to a point in my career when I was not meeting any standards physically and was in the worst shape of my life. **I constantly struggled with my self-worth and had no desire to do anything about it.** I was physically, mentally, and emotionally at the lowest point of my life. When I got to the point that I began to struggle for air just trying to tie my shoes, **I knew I needed to make some changes.**

Even though my workplace has a fitness center with everything that I need to get into shape, I could not find the motivation or the will to make the changes on my own. I found myself reaching out to friends and co-workers, telling them about how I was feeling and where I was in life. That's when I learned about this life-altering fitness program designed for first responders that piqued my curiosity. A co-worker spoke about a gym that his brother-in-law was going to and it had a program that sounded like what I was looking for. I told him that I was willing to go if he was.

On 29 October 2015, I experienced another life-altering event. That was the day I joined the Fit First Responders Program. The first thing I thought was, What did I get myself into? I hadn't felt like that since basic training. I couldn't walk right for a week, but the program had the motivation I was looking for and needed. I had never experienced anything like it. All that I had to do was walk through the door, do the workout that was on the whiteboard, and give everything I had.

In the last year, I've had so many improvements it's hard to name them all. **Physically, I'm in the best shape that I've been in for years.** I get compliments from people I haven't seen in a while. My clothes fit better, my eating habits have changed, **my self-esteem is back,** and **I am no longer taking pills for high cholesterol.** In my entire life, I would have never thought I would look forward to waking up at 0630 in the morning and going to the gym. It keeps me focused on where I'm at in life and where I don't ever want to go back to.

I cannot thank the whole coaching staff enough at FFR for all of the times they have pushed me to finish strong and given me the opportunity and tools to find the motivation in life that I was looking for.

Kenny F Butler

SSG USARMY NG OKARNG

CHAPTER NINETEEN

BE A BOSS

"BOSSES do what needs to be done, when it needs to be done…period!"

Coach JC

FFROnline.TV/Lesson-19

ARE YOU A BOSS? I'm a BOSS! We all want to be a BOSS! A boss is someone who is in control. "Boss" is a cool term kids use nowadays to say they are cool, they are the top dog. To me, being a BOSS simply means that you are in control, that you do what needs to be done to WIN. Period. Being a BOSS is about having a sense of urgency to MAKE THINGS HAPPEN. There is no one who knows more about having a sense of urgency than a first responder. You are first on the call in an emergency, you save lives, you have to act in split seconds to bring life to a dying situation. ARE YOU A BOSS? Do you have a sense of urgency?

Those first responders who are FIT FOR LIFE are the ones who make things happen because they possess a sense of urgency. A sense of urgency is established when something is of great importance to you; it is a necessity. You have got to have it. A lot of times this sense of urgency can bring some pressure, but if you want to do anything worthwhile, you had better learn to appreciate a little pressure. Pressure demands that you get it done. Pressure is knowing that when you wake up in the morning, you must find a way to make it happen. Pressure is lying down at night and creatively thinking of ways to make it happen.

Starting today, you need to feel that YOU being FIT FOR LIFE is a matter of life and death.

To be YOUR BEST, you will have to learn how to play under pressure. Why do some people break under pressure while others thrive? Pressure comes from within and once you understand that the only pressure you're under is that which is placed on you by yourself, you will then WIN ALL DAY. Pressure can bring out the best in you and possessing a sense of urgency can be used as a positive force to drive you to succeed.

> "Don't necessarily avoid sharp edges. Occasionally they are necessary to leadership."
>
> Donald Rumsfeld

In my own life, a lot of the things I've accomplished were due to the fact that I had a sense of urgency – I had to have or needed something. I distinctly remember when I started to develop the attitude that I would rather be dead than live a mediocre life. This attitude motivated me to go get things that I so badly desired and I was motivated to avoid the pain that comes from looking back with regret.

As a HERO, your WHY is the thing that will keep you mo-

19 BE A BOSS

tivated. You see, everything you do in life is for one of two reasons, to avoid pain or to gain pleasure. Many people are motivated by both. To be GREAT, you must be motivated to pursue that thing that will bring you pleasure and you must be motivated to avoid that thing that will bring you pain. This kind of motivation will develop in you a sense of urgency that will propel you and keep you moving in the right direction! It is when this happens, that you become a BOSS.

What motivates you? How badly do you really want it? What pains you? How badly do you want to avoid it?

You're on a mission and you will find a way to make it happen. You know why? Because you are a BOSS!

This is why I provide you with this game plan. This is not just another book that you read only when it's comfortable. Get it done, implement the game plan and be a BOSS! That's a sense of urgency. Doing what needs to be done, NOW!

Placing time limits on accomplishing things in various areas of your life will force you to establish a sense of urgency. You are creating this game plan so you can be FIT FOR LIFE. Give yourself a sense of responsibility and accountability by putting timelines on things.

Take action today and stay focused on the task at hand. Realize what is at the end of the tunnel. See the end result! How badly do you really want it? How urgent is it to you?

Today to be FIT FOR LIFE, you will develop a sense of urgency. YOU WILL BE A BOSS.

TAKE ACTION:

Visualize the end result, how badly do I want this?

What is the pain that I am I motivated to avoid?

What is the pleasure that I am motivated to gain?

What will I put timelines on in my life starting today?

WINNING CONFESSION:

I AM A BOSS. I do what I say I am going to do when I say I am going to do it. I have a sense of urgency to WIN in life. I WILL be the best version of me by developing the BOSS MENTALITY and doing what needs to be done NOW. I was born with a purpose. I am focused. I am determined. I am ready and NOW is my moment in life. Starting today, I will live my life knowing that I am VALUABLE AND WORTH IT. I AM A WINNER. I AM A HERO. I AM FIT FOR LIFE.

FIT FOR LIFE STORY:

Anna Cowdry and her daughter found Fit First Responders sparked a relationship with exercise for both!

I'm Anna Cowdrey and I've been a police officer with the Tulsa Police Department for 26 years.

I don't know what brought me to Fit First Responders the day I first came by to ask about the 25-week challenge, but it goes on the top of the five greatest moves I've has ever made. **I never dreamed in a million years that my walking into FFR that day would have such an amazing, life-changing affect on my and my daughter's lives...but it did!**

I wasn't sure who those two crazy cats (Coach JC & Coach Jaime) were but whatever they were telling me to do, it was working. **After about three weeks, I started to feel different-ly, not only physically, but mentally.** I started to take much greater notice of what went into my mouth and my daughter's mouth. I started looking at ingredients and discovering how much better my body processed the healthier food choices. Soon, I and my daughter were clean eaters because, after reading and understanding Coach JC's book, it became preposterous to eat any other way. **I wasn't interested in putting anything but healthy into my fuel tank and I sure as hell wasn't going to put it into my daughter's tank!**

What intrigued me most was Coach JC's statement, **"Just give me 25 weeks, and I'll transform your body."** I thought, I can't not accept this for $20 a month! As a single mother, it was hard to get to the gym. Actually, it was easy to get there, and I had the extra time...I just didn't WANT to. Putting my daughter in the daycare at my gym made me cringe since our time together was already so limited.

When I started at FFR, my daughter got to come with me and be right there, watching. She got to see what I did every day in my workout, and she wanted to do it too. This sparked a relationship with exercise not only for me, but for my daughter as well. FFR became a part of our family...a way of life for us. Being around such a positive environment is such an amazing thing for both of us. The energy the coaches bring to the table is off the charts, and they make you want to be your best.

When I started FFR, my bulletproof vest was always so uncomfortable that at times I found myself wanting to take it off on "slow nights." This is tempting for some officers because as you gain weight, the vest becomes very uncomfortable. This is just unthinkable in this day and age! Now my vest feels amazing and I would not consider going without it, even for a second.

In the middle of my 25-week challenge, I found the gun belt that I had worn for over 25 years was literally falling off of me, and I couldn't safely wear it anymore. I had to get a belt that was six inches smaller than what I had been wearing. These results blew me away! I was hooked for life.

FFR, Coach JC, and his entire staff changed my daughter's and my life, and for that, **I am eternally grateful!!**

Anna Cowdrey

Police Officer

CHAPTER TWENTY

YOU'RE NOT TIRED!

"Winners choose to not go by how they
feel at the moment, but rather take
action to get what they want!"

Coach JC

FFROnline.TV/Lesson-20

YOU'RE NOT TIRED! This is a line you will hear me say (or yell) many times throughout the day when coaching our finest and bravest first responders.

If you truly want to be FIT FOR LIFE, then you have got to start to see yourself as a WINNER, as the HERO that you are, and not allow your emotions to dictate how you act. So many times in life we make the decision to not give 100% effort because of how we feel at the moment. Your feelings are real; it's what you choose to do with them that matters. We all have a comfort zone that we try to stay in... that area that is comfortable and feels good. When life gets uncomfortable, we do whatever it takes to get ourselves back to that safe place, that comfort zone. I have seen many first responders allow this comfort zone to limit their momentum and sabotage their success. Not you! Not any longer!

To be FIT FOR LIFE, you MUST get comfortable with being uncomfortable. You must discipline yourself to not go by how you feel. YOU'RE NOT TIRED! You are not tired in life and you are not tired on the job.

"YOU'RE NOT TIRED" is a constant reminder to discipline yourself on the job, in your marriage, as a parent, in the gym, and in all areas of life to not go by how you feel. Starting today, you will make the decision to not go by how you feel. So many people don't get what they want in life because they are controlled by their emotions. So many people don't finish what they start; they quit because they don't feel like doing it at the moment.

YOU'RE NOT TIRED! You are not a quitter! The "quitter mentality" is developed when we allow ourselves to be guided by how we feel. YOUR emotions don't matter! You have a job to do! You signed an oath to be the bravest and baddest HERO in your city...YOU'RE NOT TIRED! You walked down the aisle and said, "I do"...YOU'RE NOT TIRED! You have a calling on your life and you wont stop until it is fulfilled.

> "Leaders aren't born, they are made. And they are made just like anything else, through hard work. And that's the price we'll have to pay to achieve that goal, or any goal."
>
> Vince Lombardi

One of our goals when training our first responders at FFRONLINE.tv is to provide you with at least one thing every day that will make you uncomfortable, that forces you to do something that's not easy, that you don't feel like doing at the moment. This is why I love the gym and physical training. I have seen so many first responders fight through being tired and at a low point to finish one more rep or set and then I've seen that commitment in the gym transfer over to real life. YOU'RE NOT TIRED!

Did you know that your ability is only 3% responsible for you being FIT FOR LIFE? ONLY 3%! So what's the other 97%, you ask? For you to break through, get the results you desire, create WINS, get to the next level, be THE BEST version of you and ultimately be FIT FOR LIFE, YOU HAVE TO CHOOSE TO NOT GO BY HOW YOU FEEL! You have to choose to discipline yourself…YOU'RE NOT TIRED! 97% of you getting what you really want in life is just a matter of sticking with it, never quitting, grinding it out, getting a little uncomfortable and not being moved by what you see at the moment and how you feel, but choosing to TAKE ACTION to get what you want, baby!

So are you a 3%-er?!

Today to be FIT FOR LIFE, you will choose to not go by how you feel but rather take action to get what you want. You will choose to develop the YOU'RE NOT TIRED mentality, starting today.

TAKE ACTION:

What have I started that I have given up on in life?

What am I focused on right now that I will never quit at until I get it?

What areas of my life have I become too comfortable in or burnt out in?

What will I do starting today that will be uncomfortable but necessary for me to be FIT FOR LIFE (physically, mentally, emotionally, spiritually, relationally, professionally, financially)?

WINNING CONFESSION:

I AM NOT a quitter. I WILL choose today to get outside of my comfort zone and grow by getting a little uncomfortable. I choose to create the YOU'RE NOT TIRED mentality and will not go by how I feel. Emotions do not control me. I AM action oriented and take action to get what I want in life. I AM NOT TIRED! I AM FIT FOR LIFE!

FIT FOR LIFE STORY:

Craig Coats now sees food as fuel and a tool to get him to his goals!

I'm Craig Coats and I'm a 40-year-old firefighter who has been with the Tulsa Fire Department for the last nine years. I competed in the 2015 FIT First Responders, FIT FOR DUTY. FIT FOR LIFE.

I love the teamwork and leadership at Fit First Responders, not only from the coaches who provide outstanding leadership, passion and a ton of 'give a damn,' but from everyone in there gutting it out every day! I love the opportunity to challenge others and be challenged to get through the workout and give more in other aspects of my life. I love the huddles and opportunities to hear my fellow first responders share the victories and challenges they may be facing inside and outside of the gym. I love the opportunity to say or do something that might make a difference in someone's life. I have missed leading soldiers in the Army since retiring, and this has been good therapy for me.

What keeps me coming back is the fact that, "I said I was going to do it." I love the positive atmosphere, the results, the camaraderie, the espirit de corps, and how I feel after a workout. Physically, I feel better with the nutrition and exercise. My cardio is much improved, and I have lost 20 pounds, 8% body fat, 18.3 pounds of Body Fat Mass, and 10.5 inches. I don't wear out at fires, even with the hot summer temperatures, and my deadlift max has increased over 100 pounds.

Outside of the gym, I have seen a change in how I approach my relationship with my fiancé, and I feel better prepared for getting married. My goal setting and confidence has changed, and I feel better prepared to take the Fire Equipment Operator (Drivers) promotional exam, which has been a goal of mine.

FFR has changed the way that I think about exercise, food, and life. Instead of working out just being something that I had to do to pass a physical test or get by, I think of it more as a life and death decision with that type of urgency to get ready for the next call or situation. Before, I never thought about food. I just ate and drank whatever, whenever. I hated the thought of a "diet" to follow every day, seeing it as punishment. Now I view it as fuel and as another tool to get me closer to my goals.

FFR has given me a much needed opportunity to win physically that I was missing in my life. It has helped restore my sense of pride and determination to win and the confidence that I cannot only win, but can also help others win, too.

The FFR atmosphere is positive, the results are undeniable, and we need YOU. That's right, WE NEED YOU. We need you to come and push us, inspire us, and share your story. Give us a chance to love on you and push you and make you better. We can't do it without you. **"Together we WIN."**

Craig Coates

Fire Equipment Operator / Paramedic

SECTION FIVE: CREATE THE WINNING MINDSET

CHAPTER TWENTY-ONE

ALL DAY!

"If you don't believe in yourself, why should anyone else believe in you?"

Coach JC

FFROnline.TV/Lesson-21

WIN ALL DAY! ALL DAY!

If you have spent any time around me, watched my videos, or are a part of FFRONLINE.tv, then you have heard this saying at least five times a day: "ALL DAY!" Back in 2004, I was going through a tough time in life and I came across this scripture in the Bible that says, "I can do all things through Christ who strengthens me" (Philippians 4:13). I took ahold of that word and ran with it. I started to tell myself that I can do ALL THINGS and I would say this ALL DAY. Now years later, my slogan ALL DAY has become a motivating line for many people around the world, from the athletes I have been blessed to train to the finest and bravest first responders.

Today I am going to tell you the same thing I told myself back then: ALL THINGS are possible. ALL DAY! ALL DAY is a mindset that says you expect results in all that you do. ALL DAY! It is a constant reminder that nothing is impossible to those who believe. No matter the circumstance, situation or how you feel at the moment, there is a way to WIN. ALL DAY! Dream big! Think big! Do big! ALL DAY! ALL DAY is about you, no matter what you are doing at the moment, be YOUR BEST!

ALL THINGS are possible. ALL DAY! If you are doing the things necessary to get what you desire, then you should expect results. You should expect to become FIT FOR LIFE. I always tell those HEROES who are disciplined, dedicated, determined and who put the time into training and preparing that they SHOULD EXPECT good things. You should expect results. ALL DAY!

> **"To have long term success as a coach or in any position of leadership, you have to be obsessed in some way."**
>
> Pat Riley

The mind is a powerful weapon. If you don't believe in yourself, then why should anyone else believe in you? I am not talking about being arrogant. I am talking about CONFIDENCE, a confidence that you are taking care of business, that you are back in the race, and that you are not going to quit until you reach your goal of being FIT FOR LIFE. The only one who can take you out of the game is you.

Today I want you to believe once again. Believe that ALL THINGS are possible. No matter what you are going through in life right now, start expecting results, start expecting good things, and start expecting your life to take a turn in the right direction! The time of doubting yourself is over. Expect great things to happen in your life, expect that when you put the work in, the results will come, baby. Have confidence that you can do it, will do it and you will win ALL DAY baby. Expect to be the BEST! Expect to get to the Next Level! **Expect to get what you came for!**

To be FIT FOR LIFE, you have to make that decision RIGHT NOW that you will believe that ALL THINGS are possible in your life...your health, your marriage, your financial situation, that promotion on the job...ALL DAY! Faith is believing in something you may not have at the moment. Turn your faith up, baby!

You are a HERO. Your life is valuable and before you know it, it will be over...don't waste it. You can't give up on yourself and not fulfill your destiny. Start today to remove the doubt and obstacles that are holding you back in your own mind and create the ALL DAY mentality! The ALL DAY mentality says that you will do and are doing what it takes each and every day to get what you came for to be FIT FOR LIFE. **ALL DAY is about you THINKING, SPEAKING AND ACTING as if you are already there... you are already FIT FOR LIFE.** See It, Believe It, and Expect It to come to pass.

"ALL DAY!" Say it.... Say it again.... Now say it like you mean it! ALL DAY!!!! This is your new way of building yourself up with confidence, reminding yourself that you have what it takes and nothing can stop you except you. ALL DAY! I believe in you, now believe in yourself! ALL DAY!

Today to be FIT FOR LIFE, you will adopt the ALL DAY mentality and believe that ALL THINGS are possible in your life, no matter what it looks like at the moment or how you feel.

TAKE ACTION:

What am I believing for in life?

When am I believing for this by?

What will I do to make it happen?

WINNING CONFESSION:

I choose to BELIEVE and EXPECT MORE starting today. I BELIEVE ALL THINGS ARE POSSIBLE! ALL DAY! I WILL BE MY BEST in my personal, physical, spiritual, relational and professional life. I choose to have the ALL DAY mentality and choose to do more and be more each and every day and NEVER quit. I WILL BELIEVE THAT ALL THINGS ARE POS-SIBLE. ALL DAY. I AM FIT FOR LIFE!

FIT FOR LIFE STORY:

Police Officer Dave Pyle knows no bad guys train like we do at FFR.

I'm Dave Pyle and I'm a 37-year-old police officer. I'm an FFR "OG," which means I have been with FFR since day one.

My favorite aspect of the Fit First Responders program is that my strength and conditioning just keep getting better. I have seen tremendous results physically. The many improvements in my health, conditioning, mental and emotional state are what keep me coming back to FFR.

I am finally drinking enough water and eating better than I ever have. Exercises like the prowler runs that were hard when I started are easy now. I am now at 11.3% body fat; I was at 14.2% at the beginning of FFR. I weigh in at 187 pounds, down from the 195 pounds I weighed when I started.

FFR has improved my overall health, strength, and nutrition, but my emotional health has also improved. My moods are much better and more stable since I began the challenge and got compliant with the nutrition and the 10 Habits. **I am much calmer and more patient with my family. I am calmer in high stress situations at work.**

FFR will change your life for the better. I take pride in every workout I finish. **I know that no bad guy ever trained like we do. I know I am coming home every night, because I have the strength to survive.**

David Pyle

Police Officer

CHAPTER TWENTY-TWO

TAKE BACK THE POWER

"Winning doesn't happen by chance.
Winning is a choice. Not something
you wish for, but something you
MAKE HAPPEN."

FFROnline.TV/Lesson-22

Coach JC

TAKE BACK THE POWER! Who controls your life? Who controls your actions?

I have the privilege to train some of the finest, bravest, baddest, toughest first responders in our nation. Many of these first responders, like you, have devoted their lives to the career of being a great first responder. They had a passion and fire when they graduated from the academy and entered the real world. They always desired for more in other areas of their life but like many of you, they burned out and lost their passion. Now life is not great, but at least it's comfortable. Those dreams, goals and ambitions they once had now seem like an insurmountable task. They've settled for a mediocre and complacent lifestyle not only on the job, but in other areas of their life.

You may be that first responder who has lost the fire or maybe even went through a devastating situation in life that has robbed you of your joy and passion to be FIT FOR LIFE and BE YOUR BEST. It's this kind of disconnect in a person's life – the "I'm working retired" mentality or the "I'm alive but not really living" feeling with a deep hunger to feel more alive, purposeful, and passionate - that I have seen many first responders struggle with each day.

> "You gain strength, courage and confidence by every experience in which you really stop to look fear in the face. You must do the thing you think you cannot do."
>
> Eleanor Roosevelt

Today is your day to TAKE BACK THE POWER. So many HEROES just like you suffer from this feeling of hopelessness and this delusion that their life is totally out of their control. They are bombarded with feelings that eventually create an uncomfortable vulnerability in their life. They feel that their value has been discounted, that they're not who they thought they were, and to avoid feeling this way, they turn to outlets like drugs, alcohol, overeating, gambling and even fall into a depressed state of mind. We have seen too many first responders come to us broken physically, mentally, spiritually, emotionally, financially, and relationally.

Not you! Not any longer! Today it is your day to TAKE BACK THE POWER. It is your time to take back control of your life! Shrinking back and not facing the challenges head on right now will only continue to lead you down this devastating path you are on. You may be reading this right now and thinking,

"Coach JC, my life is good." Well, I guarantee you that if you have not already, you will eventually face a time in life like this and I guarantee you that a fellow brother or sister first responder is dealing with this right now in their own life.

Let me tell you what you won't do any longer. You won't avoid the issues and hope they'll go away. We all want to avoid pain and denounce those painful emotions, but you will no longer avoid the situations that are uncomfortable in life. Stop shying away from relationships, stop avoiding church, stop feeling inadequate and get back in the gym. **YOU ARE WORTH IT!**

Today you will TAKE BACK THE POWER. Your future is in your hands. YOU ARE IN CONTROL! You will make your future happen, starting today. To TAKE BACK THE POWER, you will utilize my powerful game plan, which includes using your emotions to create the results you want so that you can live the life you desire.

Today to be FIT FOR LIFE, you will choose to TAKE BACK THE POWER by mastering your emotions and CHANGING your perspective in life.

TAKE ACTION:

5 W's TO TAKE BACK THE POWER

1. WHAT. What am I wanting to feel? How is that different from what I am feeling at the moment?

2. WRITE. Write it out. I will take time to write out and acknowledge how I feel and then I will write how I am going to choose to feel from now on.

3. WALK. Walk it out. Each day, I will stay committed to learning from my feelings, discovering a new belief about my feelings, coming to the resolution that they are not bad, and creating a solution for change.

4. WHO. Who am I rolling with? Who in my life can I be honest and real with who will support me in making this positive change? (If no one comes to mind, I will work to get that person now.)

5. WINNING. Am I WINNING? I will take time each night when I lay my head on the pillow to self evaluate, re-evaluate and check myself.

When am I believing for this by?

What will I do to make it happen?

WINNING CONFESSION:

Starting today, I WILL TAKE BACK THE POWER in my life. I AM not average and don't think like an average person. I AM not mediocre and don't do mediocre things. I walk in excellence in ALL I do, in my personal life, in my relationships, and as a HERO on the job! I WILL take action and TAKE BACK THE POWER in my emotions starting today. I AM FIT FOR LIFE.

FIT FOR LIFE STORY:

Captain Steve Rhodes is motivated by FFR to be the "Best Version of Me!"

I'm Steve Rhodes, I'm a 44-year-old Firefighter and a 20-year veteran of the Tulsa Fire Department.

My favorite aspect of Fit First Responders is the camaraderie and the fact that I am getting to know fellow first responders from the Tulsa Police, Broken Arrow Police, EMSA and Tulsa Firefighters and all surrounding cities. I've formed friendships with the coaches and my fellow first responders.

I am grateful for the coaches' genuine interest in making me and our first responders better physically and mentally. Their dedication to us is very evident when they are demonstrating exercises as well as when they are coaching us on the mental side in goal setting and staying focused.

Through FFR, I am committed to finish something when I start it. The fact that I see positive results every week (sometimes these are positive mental results) keeps me coming back. FFR has brought my fitness to the forefront. After a knee injury three years ago, I stopped running and had seen a gradual decline in my overall fitness. I have now seen my cardio improve dramatically. I have seen some muscle development and am stronger today than when I started. On the nutrition side of things, I have definitely seen a shift in my focus of what to eat and what to avoid.

Part of FFR encourages you to set goals and to prioritize things in your life, and this has been great for me. **Through FFR, I really have bought into the fact that goals have to be set to hold yourself accountable and to give direction in what you are doing.** FFR has brought a renewed interest in setting goals, encouraging me to focus on my nutrition and on sharing what I learn with my family and co-workers. **It has motivated me to be the 'Best Version of Me,' as Coach JC often says.**

I would encourage other first responders to join the FFR program. The encouragement you will receive from the FFR team and family will build your confidence. Mentally, I am more focused than I have been in a long time. I would love to see this program continue in the future in every city, not only for the positive benefits of the participants, but also for the positive benefits that I believe their families, co-workers and the citizens of the communities they proudly serve would receive.

Captain Steve Rhodes

Firefighter

CHAPTER TWENTY-THREE

FIGHT

"First we make our habits; then our habits make us."

Charles C. Noble

FFROnline.TV/Lesson-23

What are you fighting for? Are you WINNING the battles in your life? We all have our own fight in life... some of us have larger fights than others. Is your fight worth it? Are you fighting a battle that matters most in life? What are you fighting for?

Some of my favorite movies of all time are the Rocky movies. Maybe it's because I'm Italian and my boy is Sylvester Stallone... but real talk, I always loved the Rocky movies because they were comeback stories. It was a time when I could root for the underdog. We all love to see a comeback story when courage combined with hard work and perseverance prevails and defeats the guy at the top. Those kinds of characters become our HEROES in life.

Growing up, first responders - you, the police, firefighters, our military - were my HEROES. Nowadays, kids are looking to an athlete or a pop star in their search for a real life HERO due to lack of leadership and courage in our nation. But you are the HERO and starting today, it is your time to FIGHT. Have you lost your fight? Well today, it is time to take the gloves off, get back in the ring and FIGHT. In what area of your life have you been on the sideline? What areas of your life do you need to get back in the game and start fighting again?

> **"The supreme quality of leadership is integrity."**
>
> Dwight Eisenhower

You control your future, and you determine what happens now, tomorrow, and forever. You are where you are today because of the decisions you made yesterday. You will be who you are in the future based on the decisions you make today. Your physical body, your marriage, your career, your spiritual life, your financial situation... these are all your fight. Are you WINNING?

It's time to pick your battles, my friend. So many of us spend so much time fighting the wrong fight, engaged in a losing battle. I talk to so many first responders who have allowed other people and other people's situations to determine where they are in life because they got caught up in the wrong fight. It's time you take responsibility for your actions. No one forces you to do what you do and no one forces you not to do it. You are in complete control of your life, and today it's time for you to choose your battles, to choose what is worth fighting for.

Until you find that thing you are willing to die for,

you can never truly live. Until you find that WHY we spoke about earlier, that reason you do what you do, that drive, that purpose, that fire, you will continue to fight losing battles. Maybe right now you are on the brink in your marriage, maybe financially you are in danger, maybe your health is at an all time low, maybe your career is coming to an end...well, now is your time to FIGHT like your life depends on it, baby! YOU ARE A WARRIOR! Make the decision right now to never surrender. Man up! Stand up! Rise up! YOU ARE A HERO! Your family needs you, your agency needs you, your city needs you, the world needs you! GET BACK IN THE FIGHT!

You must be strong in order to FIGHT. Strong enough to overcome mental laziness and strong enough not to allow your feelings to control you. Strong enough to overcome the pressure to gossip and slander another brother. Strong enough to resist the temptation of lust and greed. Strong enough to love your spouse unconditionally, no matter what they do and say. Strong enough to lead your team and not be passive about what you stand for.

Some of you are just tired and have lost your fight. Some of you want the easy way out because you have allowed your mental laziness to create an attitude of laziness, which has produced daily laziness in your actions. Some of you have allowed your pride, ego and sense of entitlement to get in the way of you winning and now you have been knocked down and even knocked out.

Stop settling and start FIGHTING! Stop sacrificing what you want most in life for what you want at the moment! FIGHT in your FOCUS, FITNESS, FAMILY, FAITH and in your career as a firefighter HERO!

Today to be FIT FOR LIFE, you will choose to FIGHT. Starting today, you will get back in the ring and FIGHT to be FIT FOR LIFE.

TAKE ACTION:

3 P's TO WIN THE FIGHT

1. PRAYER. This is where the fight starts. I will get on my knees and surrender, knowing that I don't have to FIGHT on my own. This is my WINNING prayer: "God, I thank You for the calling on my life. I thank You for the opportunity to be a HERO. Lord, I surrender to You and ask for Your help. Father, I know that I have not been perfect and have messed up. I am truly sorry, and now I want to turn away from my past sinful life and turn toward You. Please forgive me and help me. I believe that Your Son, Jesus Christ, died for my sins, was resurrected from the dead, is alive, and hears my prayer. I invite Jesus to become the Lord of my life, to rule and reign in my heart from this day forward. Please send your Holy Spirit to guide me and help me to do Your will for the rest of my life. In Jesus' name I pray, Amen."

2. PERSISTENCE. I must possess non-stop, continual, tenacious, determined, purposeful, relentlessness. In what areas of my life will I get back in the FIGHT and be persistent?

3. PRESSURE. Today, I will turn it up and put pressure on myself to FIGHT. This is where growth happens. What actions will I choose to take each day to win the FIGHT?

WINNING CONFESSION:

I AM A WARRIOR. I AM A FIGHTER. Today, I choose to get BACK IN THE FIGHT. I am a go-getter! I AM an overcomer! I AM a mentally strong, determined, focused HERO, first responder, parent, spouse. I never settle and I can do all things. I commit to stay in PRAYER, be PERSISTENT and put PRESSURE on myself to FIGHT to WIN. I choose to take purposeful action each and every day. I WILL FIGHT! I AM FIT FOR LIFE!

FIT FOR LIFE STORY:

Jerrod Hart is leading his family to a healthier lifestyle!

I'm Jerrod Hart, and I'm a 39-year-old Sergeant with the Tulsa Police Department. I'm a Fit First Responder "OG," which means I've been with FFR from day one.

My favorite parts about Fit First Responders are the coaches and the camaraderie of the other first responders I get to train with. I like the people and the positive attitudes of everyone, how we push one another to be the best that we can be.

Since starting FFR, I have been excited about the overall change in the way I feel and I have also lost a few inches around my midsection. Every day, I feel I learn more and more about the way I should and should not eat. Also, my energy level is way better, allowing me to have more quality time with my family. **FFR has given me a greater knowledge of a healthy lifestyle.**

This lifestyle has not only helped me, but since I made the change, my family has started to follow my lead and are now living healthier lifestyles. I am a better role model for my family. I am leading my kids down a healthier path that has taken me years to get on. My kids see it working for me and are starting to want to do the things I am doing.

I stick right to the words Coach JC has said since I met him. He stated, "Everyone has a reason why, which is what they want or need." For me, my reason why is so I can lead by example. My son was born with a heart defect. God has handled my son's health, but I also needed to do my part. Also, my daughter has an autoimmune deficiency disorder, meaning her immune system is not as strong as it should be. And recently my wife was diagnosed with Postural Orthostatic Tachycardia Syndrome (POTS). **So for me, finding a healthier lifestyle wasn't just about me. I needed to do this for my family.**

My reason is to be a good example for my family and lead my kids down the right path. It's amazing how a positive healthy lifestyle rubs off. I never asked or pushed my family to take the steps I took, but since they've seen the success I am having, they are starting to take the same steps. My daughter and son have both taken the attitude that a healthier lifestyle will help their bodies and make them better athletes. They are both beating their illnesses and becoming strong, healthy kids. They are now helping other kids on their teams.

Sergeant Jerrod Hart
Police Officer

CHAPTER TWENTY-FOUR

BREAKTHROUGH

"Your BREAKTHROUGH is that
moment in time when you decide
to believe that thing you thought
was impossible, is possible!"

FFROnline.TV/Lesson-24

Coach JC

BREAK THROUGH!!

It was May 6, 1954, and no runner competing in track and field had ever run a mile in less than four minutes. All the so-called experts and commentators declared that it would never be done. Studies were performed to show that it was not humanly possible for someone to run that fast for that long in order to make it happen. For years those tests and studies stood true, and no one broke the four-minute mile barrier. However, on that day in 1954, a man named Roger Bannister made sports history and ran a mile in three minutes and fifty-nine seconds! Up until that point, the runners had allowed the opinions of others to dictate their outcome. Roger Bannister trained hard and did not believe what all the experts were saying. He did not believe that it was impossible. He refused to let others determine his outcome, and he believed that he would break the four-minute mile. He did not allow others to put a limit on his life. He was going to determine his own future and destiny.

This story is so fascinating, not only because Roger Bannister made history, but also because of what I am about to tell you: just 46 days later, another runner broke Bannister's record. Now, after more than 60 years, hundreds of runners have run a mile in less than four minutes! I want you to think about that. For hundreds of years, no one could run the mile in less than four minutes. It was pretty much accepted that no man could break the four-minute mile barrier. It was believed that a sub four-minute mile was physically impossible. It was commonly accepted as a fact! However, the reality was that the four-minute mile was a psychological barrier!

So what happened? I will tell you. For all those years, athletes allowed others to set that barrier in their minds. For all those years, runners believed what others said. Everyone was convinced that it was impossible. The lid was put on their abilities. The power of the mind is incredible! These "limiting beliefs" or "mental barriers" are real and are a lot more powerful than people give them credit for being.

> **"If I have seen farther than others, it is because I was standing on the shoulder of giants."**
>
> Isaac Newton

I am here to tell you that you can't believe everything that others are saying: the media, your family members, magazines, other books, leaders, teammates. It's time to start breaking some records. It's time to BREAK THROUGH. Change your thinking and you will change your life. It's time to create that breakthrough in your belief system concerning who you are and what you are capable of! What's your four minute mile barrier? Your BREAKTHROUGH happens to-day. Today is that moment in time when you decide to make the thing you thought was impossible, possible!

Today to be FIT FOR LIFE, you will BREAK THROUGH with my 3 B's TO BREAKTHOUGH:

1. BRAIN – What you think of the situation will deter-mine how you respond. Many times we choose to accept something that is not reality. What are you accepting men-tally? What emotions are a limiting factor in your life?

2. BELIEF – What do you believe to be true? Challenge it by asking yourself if it is reality or if you created it because you wanted to feel a certain way.

3. BLUEPRINT – What is your game plan that you will commit to execute so that you can break through?

TAKE ACTION:

What is my four-minute mile barrier in life?

What things in my thinking have been holding me back from being FIT FOR LIFE?

What will I start to believe today so that I can
BREAK THROUGH?

WINNING CONFESSION:

I choose today to BREAK THROUGH. I choose today
to create a breakthrough in my life. My mindset is strong.
I AM capable, willing and able and today, I WILL BREAK
THROUGH in my mindset. I WILL think like a WINNER.
I WILL think like a HERO. I WILL take action today and
commit to not allow any limiting beliefs to hold me back
any longer. I AM A WINNER. I AM FIT FOR LIFE.

FIT FOR LIFE STORY:

**Jeremy Jackson says without a doubt, FFR has changed
his life forever!**

I'm Jeremy Jackson and I'm a 31-year-old Tulsa Fire Department Firefighter.

My favorite part of Fit First Responders is the coaches.
**The coaches are very motivating....they are just what I
needed!** They always encourage us to do our best and
to believe in ourselves. Not only do they encourage us
to achieve our goals physically, but they encourage us to
reach our mental goals as well. I love their style of training. Each workout is custom designed to get the best results for us first responders.

When I started this program, I weighed 265 pounds.... now I'm down 30 pounds! My cardio and strength levels are increasing each week, and my stamina has improved as well. **Overall, I feel amazing!** I am addicted to the way I feel now that my body is changing and my health is improving. I crave my morning workouts. Some people need coffee. I need this workout! It helps get my day started. There is a great sense of brother/sisterhood here in the FFR family, and everyone is supportive of each other.

I feel that FFR gave me the tools I needed to be a better version of me by focusing on our four key pillars: food, family, fitness, focus - and don't forget the fifth one...faith. These five things are the core of what FFR stands for. **FFR has taught me that in order to win in life, you have to establish a winning mentality and conquer your weaknesses.** Each day I start my day thinking of how to apply FFR's five key values to my life.

Without a doubt, my life has been changed forever because of this FFR program. About two years ago, I was diagnosed with sleep apnea. After only a few weeks of training with FFR, I no longer needed to use the CPAP machine. I now sleep better and have more energy throughout the day. FFR has helped me establish a strong mindset and helped with goal setting. **I have gained confidence and a more positive self-image.**

If you want to get in the best shape of your life, both mentally and physically, then I highly recommend FFR! It is hard work, but with that comes big reward! Like Coach JC always says, "If you want something you never had, you've got to do something you've never done." FFR is like family. They are there every step of the way to encourage and motivate you. **FFR isn't just 'another place to work out'...it is a workout that puts you in place - a place that allows you to succeed, achieve, and surpass all your goals, become a better person, and a better first responder.**

Jeremy Jackson

Firefighter

CHAPTER TWENTY-FIVE

FINISH STRONG

"When we do the best that we can, we
never know what miracle is wrought
in our life, or in the life of another."

FFROnline.TV/Lesson-25

Helen Keller

You've gone the distance, baby: 25 lessons to be FIT
FOR LIFE. You have invested a tremendous amount of
time, energy, effort, sacrifice and dedication to put yourself in this position to WIN in life. Now it's time to FINISH
and FINISH STRONG! So many people start things without having the commitment to finish them...from reading
a book to being in a marriage. You will never finish if you
quit. You will never have the option to quit if you never
start. You, my friend, started this game plan and now you
are about to finish it. But this FINISH STRONG lesson is
way more than just finishing this book. It's about you FIN-
ISHING STRONG in life.

Finishing what you start is a mindset. It's making a
commitment to FINISH WHAT YOU START. It's you saying that it doesn't matter how you feel or what happens,
you are a person who finishes what they start. You don't
just finish, but you FINISH STRONG. What does that
mean, to finish strong? Ask any competitor and they will
tell you that what matters most is not how you start, but
how you finish.

What in your life have you started that you have not FINISHED STRONG? What area do you need to commit, from today forward, to FINISH STRONG in? How you do anything is how you do everything. Start today to develop the "I AM A FINISHER" attitude. In ALL that you do, determine that your effort will be 100% until the end. Practice doesn't make perfect...PERFECT practice makes perfect. Starting today, practice FINISHING STRONG in all that you do. This will build endurance in your life. This will then transfer over to the larger things in life so that you can produce more WINS.

Your window of opportunity is small and you must maximize each day. This always makes me think of my favorite movie, Rocky III. In Rocky III, when Rocky is training, Apollo Creed reminds him that there is no tomorrow. Live today like it's your last. Give it ALL you've got, as you are never promised tomorrow! If you want to be motivated, Google that Rocky clip. It gets me hyped every time.

Now I want to give you a game plan for HOW TO FINISH STRONG:

1. FOCUS ON "BREAKING THROUGH THE FINISH LINE." Many of you are extremely talented at what you do, but regardless of your talent, effort and hard work, you still seem to not be able to finish on top. No matter what you do, you still feel like you're losing! Consistently placing second or sometimes not even placing at all, trying over and over to win with nothing working, eventually makes you grow frustrated. This might be the way you felt 25 weeks ago or even today. Starting today, FINISHING STRONG is who you are and what you do. FINISHING STRONG is committing to keep the intensity as high as possible until you break through the finish line. Stop looking over your shoulder to see who is behind you...past failures, mistakes, limiting thoughts, what someone told you as a kid... NO MORE! NOW IT'S TIME to focus only on the end... on breaking through the finish line. Forget what has happened behind you. **Winners choose to not focus on the past but keep their eyes focused on the prize.**

When you continue to look over your shoulder at the past, you shift your attention from the positive goal of winning to the possibility of failing again or the fear of being mediocre or of someone overtaking you. When you allow your thoughts to go this direction, it affects your action and slows you down.

> **"Don't go around saying the world owes a living. The world owes you nothing. It was here first."**
>
> Mark Twain

When you focus your THOUGHTS only on BREAKING THROUGH THE FINISH LINE and FINISHING STRONG, your brain is telling your body to not quit. You no longer think about what is behind you, but you stay FOCUSED on the victory that is awaiting you!

2. VICTORY IS WON OR LOST IN THE FINAL YARDS. All your hard work over the last 25 lessons can be thrown away in the final moments. Do not grow weary. Do not quit. Your victory comes with those last few reps, the last few minutes before your kids go to bed, the last few moments you spend with your spouse before you head off to shift. The game is won or lost in the last few yards... FINISH STRONG.

3. FOCUS ONLY ON ONE THING, BREAKING THROUGH THE FINISH LINE. Some people are ok with just finishing what they start. I am all about you finishing, but I want you to finish by breaking through. I want for you to finish with a feeling of accomplishment, a feeling of pride, with excitement in knowing that you just didn't finish but you FINISHED STRONG. BREAK THROUGH those last few moments, those last few yards, those last few reps so that you can WIN.

TODAY to be FIT FOR LIFE, you will choose to FINISH AND FINISH STRONG.

TAKE ACTION:

In what area of my life have I dropped out of the race? (Be specific)

In what areas of my life will I start today to FINISH STRONG so that I can build endurance?

What do I see at the finish line (what victory am I FINISH-ING STRONG for)?

WINNING CONFESSION:

I AM A WINNER. I FINISH WHAT I START. I CHOOSE TODAY TO DEVELOP THE FINISH STRONG MENTALITY. I am not a quitter. I WILL live today as if it were my last and enjoy every moment. I choose to create fun in my life and run my race. I WILL CREATE BREAKTHROUGHS IN MY LIFE BY FINISHING STRONG! I am FIT FOR LIFE!

FIT FOR LIFE STORY:

Luke Flanagan feels stronger, lighter, happier and more confident since joining FFR!

I'm Luke Flanagan and I'm a 28-year-old Tulsa Police Officer.

It is impossible to name just one favorite thing about Fit First Responders. I love the passion and enthusiasm that Coach JC and the other coaches have for each individual in the program. I also love the camaraderie between Police, Fire National Guard and EMSA.

In the five years that I have been a police officer, I haven't experienced anything like it...oh yeah, did I mention I love the results?

The results that I have seen are what keep me coming back. In the first 11 weeks, I lost just over 20 pounds and am gaining muscle simultaneously. I also increased my flexibility and have far less lower back pain. But the results are not only physical, but mental and spiritual as well. I feel stronger, lighter, happier, and more confident than I've felt in years. I also value the new relationships that I've built with other first responders.

Fit First Responders has pushed me to become a better husband and a better father. I have been pushed to make healthier decisions so I can have many more years to spend with my wife and kids. The more weight that I lose, the more energy that I gain.

I know taking the first step is the hardest, but once you begin seeing the results and get your mind right, it is impossible to quit. In the short amount of time that I have been a part of FFR, I have seen and felt more results than in years of trying to do it on my own. There is definitely strength in numbers.

Luke Flanagan
Police Officer

> "If you want something you've never had, you have to do something you've never done."

Coach JC

Congratulations! You did it! You completed your 25-lesson FIT FOR LIFE game plan so that you can create the WINNING Mindset and WIN as a first responder and WIN in life!

The principles that you have just read are simple, and they work if you just work them. Once you transform your thinking and create the WINNING mindset, you will have the FIT FOR LIFE lifestyle and be YOUR BEST.

The choice is yours, my friend! Remember, success is not some big event that just happens. It comes down to you executing your daily action steps and exercising the law of WINNING in your life. No one else can do it for you. Time can work for you or against you! OWN THE MOMENT and GET WHAT YOU CAME FOR.

I believe in you and know that you desperately want to be FIT FOR LIFE. Listen to me, don't get overwhelmed, just follow the game plan and execute that one simple, disciplined thing every day that will get you to the promise land!

So, where do you go from here? You go back to page one of this book and you evaluate every day to assure that you are executing the game plan. You use this book as a blueprint. Revisit the lessons, action steps and winning confessions so that you can continue to grow.

Now is your time to take it to the NEXT LEVEL. We created an online community just for first responders to be

FIT FOR DUTY. FIT FOR LIFE. Every day, we give you a WINNING game plan with mental conditioning, nutritional coaching, online workouts for all fitness levels and an online community where first responders can hold each other accountable and have fun as together we WIN IN LIFE.

Get over to www.FITFIRSTRESPONDERS.com and start your 7 day FREE trial.

YOU ARE...
FIT FOR DUTY. FIT FOR LIFE.

Coach JC

I WOULD LOVE TO HEAR FROM YOU!

I know this book has changed your life! I would love to hear from you. Please write to me as I would love to hear how it impacted you in being FIT FOR DUTY. FIT FOR LIFE.

Contact me! Send letters to:
Coach JC Enterprises
8177 S Harvard Ave., Suite 420
Tulsa, OK 74137

email or call us:
1-800-382-1506
info@coachjc.com
info@fitfirstresponders.com

www.CoachJC.com
www.FitFirstResponders.com

ARE YOU READY TO BE FIT FOR DUTY & FIT FOR LIFE?

GET YOUR ONLINE WORKOUTS FOR FIRST RESPONDERS ANYWHERE, ANYTIME.

WHAT IS FFR ONLINE?

FFR Online Is A Community Built Only For First Responders With The Tools You Need To Be Fit For Duty, Fit For Life.

FITNESS
Daily workouts specifically for first responders for ALL fitness levels.

FOCUS
Daily mental conditioning to be your BEST on and off the job.

FOOD
Daily habits on how to eat to perform and look your best.

FAMILY
The ONLY online community for first responders.

WHAT DO I GET WITH MY MEMBERSHIP?

- ⊘ DAILY WORKOUTS
- ⊘ DAILY NUTRITION COACHING
- ⊘ DAILY MENTAL CONDITIONING
- ⊘ ONLINE COMMUNITY
- ⊘ A CHANCE TO WIN A BRAND NEW TRUCK
  AND MUCH MORE…

BECOME A FIT FIRST RESPONDER TODAY
$25 PER MONTH. YOUR FIRST 7 DAYS ARE FREE.
SIGN UP NOW AT: WWW.FITFIRSTRESPONDERS.COM

FFR IS A NON PROFIT 501 (C) (3)ORGANIZATION - ALL DONATIONS GO BACK TO SERVE YOUR FELLOW HEROES.

ABOUT JONATHAN CONNEELY

COACH JC

Coach JC, America's #1 Life Success Coach, is an author, entrepreneur, motivational speaker, life coach, and one the top strength and conditioning coach in the nation.

Coach JC has been empowering people to WIN for over 15 years by coaching them to overcome obstacles, breakthrough limitations and create "The Winning Mindset." Coach JC has been privileged to train people from all walks of life through his private life coaching and motivational speaking.

Coach JC started his career at the Division 1 level at Oral Roberts University training athletes and later launched Tulsa's premier sports performance facility, Dynamic Sports Development. Coach JC started Tulsa's first ever outdoor fitness program for women, Bootcamp Tulsa and is the founder of The Secret to Real Weight Loss Success for Christians, an 8-week body transformation program in the churches across America. Coach JC authored the book series: *The Secret to Real Success, The Secret to Real Weight-loss Success* and *The Secret to Real Athlete Success.*

Coach JC founded nonprofit Fit First Responders after seeing a need to help first responders win in their fitness, nutrition and in life to perform better on and off the job to keep America's city streets safe.

To learn more about Coach JC please visit:

LinkedIn: Jonathan Conneely

Facebook: Coach JC

Twitter: @Coach_JC

Instagram: THECOACHJC

www.COACHJC.com

ABOUT FIT FIRST RESPONDERS

Fit First Responders (FFR) is a nonprofit dedicated to empowering police officers, firefighters, medics, and National Guard to WIN in their physical and mental health so they can be FIT FOR DUTY and FIT FOR LIFE to keep America's city streets safe. Fit First Responders physical training, mental conditioning, spiritual guidance, and life coaching has help thousands of our Nations first responders be their best on and off the job.

Fit First Responders is a non-profit that relies solely on corporate sponsors and individual donors to support YOU, the finest and the bravest, so we can provide YOU the BEST physical and mental training in the country. If you know someone who would be a good partner, please email us at info@fitfirstresponders.org or give us a call at 1(800) 382 1506. To learn more about FFR, visit our website at **www.FITFIRSTRESPONDERS.org.**

REQUEST COACH JC FOR YOUR AGENCY

 Jonathan Conneely, Coach JC, is available for speaking engagements at conferences, departments and agencies.

ORGANIZATIONS BRING IN COACH JC TO SPEAK ON THE TOPICS OF:

Leadership | Teamwork
Motivation | Culture Development
Mental Conditioning
FIT FOR DUTY. FIT FOR LIFE.

TO MAKE COACH JC A PART OF YOUR AGENCY, DEPARTMENT OR EVENT PLEASE CONTACT US AT:

1-800-382-1506
email: info@coachjc.com

www.CoachJC.com
www.FitFirstResponders.org

We look forward to helping your team be
FIT FOR DUTY. FIT FOR LIFE.

Our Father who art in heaven,

hallowed be thy name.

Thy kingdom come.

Thy will be done on earth

as it is in heaven.

Give us this day our daily bread,

and forgive us our trespasses,

as we forgive those who trespass against us,

and lead us not into temptation,

but deliver us from evil.

For thine is the kingdom,

and the power, and the glory,

for ever and ever.

Amen.